radicalgraphicsradicals

hicsradicals

by

LAUREL HARPER

Foreword by

MARVIN SCOTT JARRETT

Preface by

KATHERINE MCCOY

CHRONICLE BOOKS

SAN FRANCISCO

Text ©1999 by
LAUREL HARPER

Library of Congress Cataloging-in-Publication Data:
Harper, Laurel.
Radical graphics/graphic radicals/by Laurel Harper;
foreword by Marvin Scott Jarrett; preface by Katherine McCoy.
            p. cm.
Includes bibliographical references.
ISBN 0-8118-1680-X (hc)
1. Graphic arts—History—20th century. 2. Commercial art—
History—20th century. I. Title.
NC998.4.H37 1999   98-49144
741.6'09'045—dc21   CIP

Printed in Hong Kong.

Design by
KATHERINE MCCOY, with ERIN SMITH and JANICE PAGE

Distributed in Canada by
RAINCOAST BOOKS
8680 Cambie Street, Vancouver, British Columbia V6P 6M9

10 9 8 7 6 5 4 3 2 1

CHRONICLE BOOKS
85 Second Street, San Francisco, California 94105

www.chroniclebooks.com

table of contents

Foreword Sharing the Vision by MARVIN SCOTT JARRETT 6

Preface Risky Business by KATHERINE MCCOY 9

Acknowledgments 10

Introduction Radical Roots 11

Section 1 Mentors 33

PIERRE BERNARD, Atelier de Création Graphique 34

NEVILLE BRODY, Research Studios 38

ART CHANTRY, Art Chantry Studio 42

JUST DESIGN, Spencer Drate and Jütka Salavetz 46

EMIGRE, Zuzana Licko and Rudy VanderLans 50

ED FELLA, California Institute of the Arts 54

TIBOR KALMAN, M&Co. Labs, Inc. 58

KATHERINE MCCOY, McCoy & McCoy 62

PAULA SCHER, Pentagram 66

RICK VALICENTI, Thirst 70

Section 2 Innovators 75

BOELTS BROS. ASSOCIATES,
Jackson Boelts, Eric Boelts, Kerry Stratford 76

MARGO CHASE, Margo Chase Design 80

THE DESIGNERS REPUBLIC, Ian Anderson, Mike Place,
Nick Bax, Matt Pyke, Dave Bailey, Liz Close, Julia Parfitt 86

JAGER DI PAOLA KEMP DESIGN,
Michael Jager, Giovanna Di Paola, David Kemp 92

MAX KISMAN, Max Kisman Design 96

REBECA MÉNDEZ,
Rebeca Méndez Communication Design 100

MODERN DOG DESIGN CO.,
Robynne Raye and Michael Strassburger 106

REVERB, Somi Kim, Lisa Nugent, Susan Parr 110

CARLOS SEGURA, Segura Inc. and [T-26] 116

STUDIO MD, Glenn Mitsui, Jesse Doquilo, Randy Lim 122

PAUL SYCH, Faith 126

VSA PARTNERS, Dana Arnett, Robert Vogele,
James Koval, Curt Schreiber, Ken Schmidt 130

MARTIN VENEZKY, Appetite Engineers 134

WHY NOT ASSOCIATES,
David Ellis, Andrew Altmann, Patrick Morrissey 140

CRAIG YOE, Yoe! Studio 146

Section 3 Progeny 151

CHRIS ASHWORTH, Substance 152

BRAND DESIGN CO., Rich Roat, Andy Cruz, Allen Mercer 156

SCOTT CLUM, Rid e Design 160

JERÔME CURCHOD, Ray Gun Publishing 164

CYAN, Detlef Fiedler, Daniela Haufe, Sophie Alex 168

AMY FRANCESCHINI, Futurefarmers 174

FUSE, Rich Godfrey 178

GALIE JEAN-LOUIS, MSNBC 182

GEOFF KAPLAN, General Working Group 186

POST TOOL DESIGN, Gigi Biederman and David Karam 192

STEFAN SAGMEISTER, Sagmeister, Inc. 198

LEE SCHULZ, California Institute of the Arts 202

SMAY VISION, Stan Stanski and Phil Yarnall 206

GAIL SWANLUND, Swank Design 210

GIULIO TURTURRO, Verve Records 216

Selected Bibliography 220

Art Credits 222

sharing the vision

MARVIN SCOTT JARRETT, FOUNDER, RAY GUN PUBLISHING

I have always had great respect for the power of graphic design in helping define a product's unique personality and in reaching out to audiences. Though I never wanted to become a designer—I see myself in the macro sense rather than the micro—I grew up with a surfing buddy who was a graphic designer and he introduced me to design's potency. I would pore over his design annuals, fascinated by what I saw. So when I decided to put everything on the line and start a magazine, I knew success would depend a lot on establishing a fifty-fifty relationship between great visual and great editorial content. And, since my publication would be a music lifestyle magazine aimed at young, forward-thinking readers, I knew its look had to be something edgy that would stand out from the clutter.

I had tried to start my first magazine—another music publication—while in junior high school, with the help of a friend. We produced it from my bedroom, printing it on an old photocopier. We were only thirteen-year-old kids, so the magazine had no look and never really got off the ground. But the idea stuck in the back of my mind. One thing led to another until, years later, I was working at the music magazine *Creme* and got my chance. The owner was an accountant in his late fifties who had bought the magazine as an investment and eventually put it into suspended publication. I got an old friend of mine to back me financially and we bought the title. One of the first things I did was search for a designer who could give *Creme* a visual identity that matched my concept for its voice. I combed through design annuals like *Print* and *Communication Arts*, looking at whose work attracted me and whom I thought might share my vision of where *Creme* should be. That's how I found GARY KOEPKE. He understood what I wanted to achieve with the magazine and I respected his ability to get me there.

That was the start of a long and lucrative relationship with Gary, as well as with many other graphic designers who aren't afraid to buck the system to achieve a singular presence. Since working with Gary on *Creme*, I've paired up with DAVID CARSON on *Ray Gun*, and now with JÉRÔME CURCHOD, the magazine's current art director; with P. SCOTT MAKELA, LAURIE HAYCOCK-MAKELA, and JERÔME CURCHOD on *Sweater*; with SCOTT CLUM on *Stick*; and with PAUL VENUS on *Bikini*. I've also worked on independent projects with other great artists such as VAUGHAN OLIVER (whom the British Consulate has called the "premier UK designer" for his work for the record label *4AD*, and for his poster designs and television station and video titles) and TERRY JONES, designer of England's *ID* magazine. Though each is a distinct personality, they all share one trait: they strive to connect with their audiences in ways that, when viewed from a so-called traditional design stance, may be far-fetched, but when taken from a communications standpoint are right on target.

I want whoever buys one of my magazines to pick it up and go, *"Wow! This is cool. I've gotta have it."* I want the person to experience the magazine's tactility, to be enticed to open it up, look at the pages, and keep it. I want the reader to show it off on his or her coffee table, to elevate it to collectible status. With strong competition from the likes of MTV, video games, and Web sites, getting someone to take the time to look at a two-dimensional piece of paper isn't easy anymore. It must be impressive. That's why design is so important.

Relaxing control of your product takes courage on the client's part. It means allowing designers the latitude to experiment and do something different. It also takes courage on the designer's part to strive for something new. But why create the same thing that someone else is already doing? The way I work is I have a vision in my head, then I look for a designer to bring it to concrete reality. My vision is a lot more cloudy than what will ultimately be developed, and so within that bigger picture I allow the designer a tremendous amount of freedom. Granted, when you turn a graphic designer loose there is a certain anxiety. But it has always compensated me to the utmost degree. The trick is, find a designer whom you connect with, then allow that person freedom to do what you hired him or her to do.

I want to work with people who will give me something they really believe in, something that is special. In exchange for this freedom, designers have rewarded me with products that are more like pieces of modern art than commercial mishmash. It's the difference between producing a product that we all can be proud of versus something homogeneous and mundane.

If I were asked by another businessperson for one piece of advice on how to succeed, it would be this: make certain that your designer knows the audience you want to reach, then heed what he or she has to say, even if it is a bit scary and means stretching beyond the known. Think of the designer as someone who can bring value to your effort. If you view your designer only as a vendor, that is the kind of output you will get. If you consider your designer a partner in your business, you're a lot farther along the road to achieving your goals.

So let the critics call what we produce Radical. I call it good business sense. And I call it exciting. That, to me, is a lot more important than maintaining the status quo.

risky business

KATHERINE MCCOY, MCCOY & MCCOY

Information architect/design critic RICHARD SAUL WURMAN has pointed out that walking is extremely risky business. With each step forward, one must momentarily lose balance and assume an unstable position before landing on the other foot. Being a graphic designer is like this.

It also strikes me that if one believes in design truisms, absolute paradigms applicable to any time and any audience—for instance, the universal truths sought by the Bauhaus—then change is a negative design value. But I find it hard to believe that we already know all there is to know about design. I am constantly looking for new methods and forms to integrate into my personal design process. Because I am a pluralist, this puts me at odds with purists—those who want to find "the right way" and stick with it—and puts me on the side of progressive change rather than fixed permanence. I would not find a profession very interesting in which all methodology had been completely codified with nothing left for discovery.

Change can be evolutionary or revolutionary—incremental and progressive or cataclysmic and abrupt. I am more comfortable with evolutionary change, a continual building, rather than creating something that's a rejection of everything that has come before. But I also find an occasional thunderbolt in either my or a colleague's work very stimulating. This is not the same thing as chasing the trend of the season, the tendency in graphic design to perpetually search for novel styles. The change I am interested in is not change for change's sake, but is about growth and the advancement of design's body of knowledge. If this is Radical, so be it!

Dedicated to the memories of TIBOR KALMAN and P. SCOTT MAKELA, whose creative passions epitomized the spirit of graphic radicals everywhere.

acknowledgments

I want to thank everyone who made this book possible, including my husband, GEORGE, who kept me pointed in the right direction; my parents, BOB and JOANN HOSKINS, who never let me forget when I was past deadline; my editorial assistant, AARON FEWELL, for keeping me organized and lending a much-needed hand; editor ALAN RAPP for being so patient and for his valuable input, along with copyeditor JEFF CAMPBELL; and KATHY MCCOY for her guidance and moral support, and, particularly, for making this book's countenance sing.

I also want to thank all those people in design studios who put aside their other duties to provide me with information and artwork. Especially, however, I am indebted to the many Radical talents across the world who so vigorously search for new ways to communicate and, as a result, have injected the design profession with such energy, excitement, and passion.

introduction

radical **roots**

Graphic designer RICK THARP was once asked by *HOW* magazine (February 1996) to itemize the ten best and worst things that had happened in his profession from 1985 to 1995. Occupying the number two spot on both lists was the fact that DAVID CARSON, ZUZANA LICKO, RUDY VANDERLANS, and RICK VALICENTI were designing during that period.

Paul Sych, *Our Father, Who's Art Is in Heaven?,* 1997.

This self-promotion piece by Paul Sych of Faith, Toronto, leaves few previously taboo subjects untouched. The designer proclaims his faith in design in a controversial manner that is imbued with the three main Radical traits: self-expression, innovation, and exploration.

The four are major players in a controversial design genre driven by a fusion of **dauntless exploration**, **seditious innovation**, and **passionate self-expression**. They seem determined to ignore or undermine the establishment's view of good design, foregoing the **traditional rules** of legibility, orderly grids and columns, and logical information flow. In their work, **text** is often used as **imagery** rather than mere words whose sole purpose is to deliver a message; inserting **personal** artistic work, a taboo of many traditional designers, is frequently a prime goal. The design itself becomes a part of, rather than merely a vehicle for, the message.

While their work has been called everything from Next Wave and Deconstructionist to "garbage," "Radical" seems the most appropriate label for this pioneering, yet inflammatory group. This is not a formal movement—indeed, a number of Radical designers balk at being labeled as anything other than **individualists**—but there is a common aesthetic and philosophy that unites them. In the thesaurus, synonyms for radical include *passionate*, *revolutionary*, *intense*, and *progressive* as well as *rabid*, *fanatical*, *fiend*, and *nut*. This **diversity** of adjectives is as good a place to start as any: it is a succinct description of the Radicals and offers great insight into why they provoke such intense feelings, both of praise and criticism.

The Radicals probably have been denunciated more than any other group in the history of design. Many traditional designers, especially those attached to the Swiss school, have been especially vocal in their disdain. The **Swiss** (or International Typographic) style developed in Switerzerland after World War II, growing out of

Cyan, Manifesto of the Communist Party, *1995.*

Cyan, a Berlin studio, firmly adheres to the overlapping

of life and art. This ideology closely links its members with

the avant-garde artists of the 1920s and early 1930s.

the work of the Russian Constructivists, De Stijl, the Bauhaus, and the New Typography of the 1930s. It prescribes refined, uncluttered, grid-driven arrangements, an orderly sense of balance to the composition, clean white space, and clearly legible typefaces (predominantly Helvetica). The main objective of this school of thought is to present information in a **structured**, **rational** manner.

During the late 1970s, the Swiss style became increasingly identified with **corporate design**, particularly in the United States. MASSIMO VIGNELLI, a founding partner in 1965 of the international design firm Unimark, and later, in 1971, of Vignelli Associates, New York, was a leading proponent of the Swiss style. It comes as no surprise then that he was among the most vocal of the Radicals' critics, probably the first to label it "**garbage**" design. *"We cannot put garbage on a pedestal; just because it exists does not prove it is quality,"* he contended in a much-debated article that appeared in *Print* magazine (issue 5, 1991). Even the late PAUL RAND—though considered a design rebel for his avant-garde work of the 1940s and 1950s in which he simultaneously sought to solve communication problems while satisfying a need for personal expression—was moved to write the book *Design Form and Chaos* (Yale University Press, 1993) in an attempt to chastise the Radicals and restore a sense of **order** to the profession. What such traditionalists tend to downplay or overlook altogether is the Radicals' role as another test tube in the **laboratory** of design innovation.

It's no wonder that the Radicals upset those who believe that design's mission is only as a **facilitator** of messages; no Radical would confine his or her work to such a narrow premise. Radical designs are often hard to read or outright illegible, depending on whom you talk to, and they require **involvement** on the part of the viewer to comprehend. Most Radicals design for a specific audience in a **specific context**, and they reject the notion that it is possible for everyone, regardless of age, gender, culture, and background, to respond to and understand the same design vernacular in the same manner. *"We design not for future historians to judge or condemn, but for an audience with immediate needs and expectations,"* PHIL BAINES wrote in the British design publication *Eye* (issue 7, 1992). After years of struggling to convince the business world that design is a respectable marketing tool, many conservative designers consider the Radicals' work and their insistence on **subjectivity** an undermining evil.

Zuzana Licko and Rudy VanderLans, *Emigre* #32, fall 1994. *Zuzana Licko and Rudy VanderLans of Emigre Studio, Sacramento, California, pioneered digital letterforms. Initially, the two purchased a Macintosh simply to replace the typewriter on which they did their "typesetting" for their publication Emigre. Licko became fascinated with the primitive, bitmapped typefaces she could create on the computer. VanderLans started showing off his partner's work in Emigre, and the magazine soon emerged as the voice of the computer-design generation. Shown here is an article created by guest designer Gail Swanlund.*

Or so goes the ideology, of the post-industrial military complex.

ROUTE 66   **It's no mistake**

that the metaphor of a highway is used for the "Information Superhighway." Just as the roots of much of the computer technologies lie in the military, so the interstates were funded and built following World War II, for "national security." One of the distinguishing design parameters, for example, was the ability to handle tank traffic.

Route 66 is among the most fondly remembered icons of a squeaky clean America. You know, the black-and-white, mostly white, America where justice always prevailed in old Perry Mason episodes. It of course lies in ruin now, abandoned in favor of the faster nonstop interstates. But while Route 66 was built as part of a military agenda, it was also the path for something else that consumed America: the Dream West ideal, the hope for a better future, for unbounded possibilities, the American dream taken to its western fringe. For Route 66 simply concretized in modern asphalt the wagon train paths to the west. The Chicago-to-LA road still exists in driveable fragments, its rusting vernacular signage a veritable encyclopedia of American Mythos: the land of cowboys and Indians, the Grand Canyon, cheap petrol and winged horses, and early nuclear test sites. That was back when we had a good deal of hope for a bright future, which we pinned (or had pinned for us) onto the nuclear enterprise.

That American dream soured, turning instead into an irrelevant dystopia. The Hopi, whose lands are now horrific sites of uranium mines and cardboard and scrap metal "houses," recall their 2,000 year old (probably more ancient) prophecy that pretty much describes "spiderwebs in the sky" and a nuclear apocalypse in vivid detail. Snoopy's scruffy uncle, Spike, comes out of the desert, out of the city Needles every so often, looking as though he had more to do with the city's name (we're not talking cactus here) than what Charles Schultz had in mind. It was aptly named though, as the last town one hits before the LA megapolis. The City of Angels often shows up on our TV screens now with little reference to wide boulevards lined with palm trees, beach parties, and glamorous movie stars that characterized it from the days of early cinemas to the recent past. Our contemporary images are of smog, endless traffic, earthquakes, a city afire with "racial unrest." Like the question put to the replicant in "Blade Runner," LA's historically seemy underside lies like the struggling turtle, belly-up, baking in the blazing Mohave sun. Where mom and pop restaurants lined Route 66, mini-malls and McDonalds now replace them, quality assured, or absurd.

I dreamed of getting my kicks on Route 66, for it represented an America that is forever out of my reach in the Never-Never Land of being a hyphenated American, the product of emigre parents, someone strung out between the yuppies, who gave the promise of capital one more abusive kick, with the supposed lost Generation X. For all of their engaging accents and old world charm, my parents, addicted to relentless CNN broadcasts in their retirement, find America always obscene, an obscenity I revel in. But I take comfort in their salty, smelly fish in the same way I take perverse comfort in the safe sterility of the McDonalds' oases, one of this country's most effective of melting pots, homogenizing the hell out of any purported diversity, doing in America what Coke does globally.

David Carson, *Ray Gun*, 1993.

The eclectic design of Ray Gun *is as popular with its readers as the articles. The alternative music magazine promulgated the "garbage look" in design, inspiring not only other publications aimed at the Gen-X audience but more traditional marketing vehicles such as print ads and television graphics.*

Perhaps most unsettling to critics is what has been a main catalyst behind the Radicals' work—the Macintosh **computer** and its onslaught of software (Aldus PageMaker, QuarkXPress, Adobe Illustrator, and Adobe Photoshop, most notably). The advent of the computer in design studios during the mid-1980s for the first time allowed users to quickly, easily, and, as such, sometimes uncontrollably pile icon upon icon, stretch type far beyond legibility, and distort images to obscene proportions. The results were bold and frequently ugly, especially in the eyes of many traditionally trained artists. They charge that the Radical look, then and now, is formulated more by **technology** than by any sense of **aesthetic**. And in fact, the computer has helped democratize the modern design world, allowing people with little or no formal training to hang up their shingles and begin designing.

But mediocre work and ignorant practitioners are not just the bane of the digital Radicals; every design era produces some awful work, a lot of average, a bit of good, and an iota of outstanding. Some critics make no distinction between designers of whatever level of training who get caught up in the bells and whistles of digital wizardry and those Radicals in control who are cogently exploring the **new terrain** that computers lay before them.

Emigre's LICKO and VANDERLANS are prime examples of designers whose work runs the gamut of criticism. Licko was among the first to recognize the aesthetic potential of the Macintosh when it was introduced in 1984. She was particularly fascinated by the quirkiness of the computer's **low-resolution** typefaces and set about creating new faces on the Macintosh by playing off the letterforms' primitive, pixeled attributes. VANDERLANS then disseminated his partner's creations via his own revolutionary digital explorations in the pages of *Emigre* magazine. Some called their work **genius**; others, such as VIGNELLI, who was referring specifically to *Emigre* magazine in the *Print* article, labeled it digital **bunk**.

The same love/hate reactions have been generated by DAVID CARSON's eclectic chaos in two publications: the short-lived *Beach Culture*, a magazine for surfers and beach enthusiasts that was published from 1991 to 1992, and *Ray Gun*, an alternative music magazine launched in 1993. Both publications sorely test readers' **patience** by forcing them to follow layered text that is subject to run off the page, bleed into black holes, or simply stop midsentence, among other visual **aberrations**. Carson began planning his designs with the idea that there were better ways to communicate with the magazines' young audiences than to follow the clean, grid-heavy, cookie-cutter look adopted by many publications in the late 1980s and early 1990s. Judging from the reaction, particularly in the case of *Ray Gun*, Carson is right. *"Ray Gun may actually get young people reading again,"* USA Today said. Even *Newsweek* magazine (February 26, 1996) and the *New York Times* (May 14, 1994) were impressed, paying attention to a profession largely ignored by the general press and featuring Carson within their venerable pages.

Still, many conservative designers refused to recognize Carson's work as anything other than that of a **naive phenom** (he was educated as a sociologist rather than a designer) whose flame would soon burn out. At one venerated design competition in the mid-1990s, when the hype on Carson was running rampant, two of the three judges refused to even look at his entries. Passions obviously run high when it comes to judging the validity of the Radicals' work.

RICK VALICENTI further fanned the fire when he packed a 1991 Gilbert Paper promotion full of artistic **self-expression**. Critics were appalled, saying Valicenti had stepped over that sacred tenuous line separating design and art. *"Why not?"* an unrepentant Valicenti counters. After all, fine art has been the major influence for many design legends.

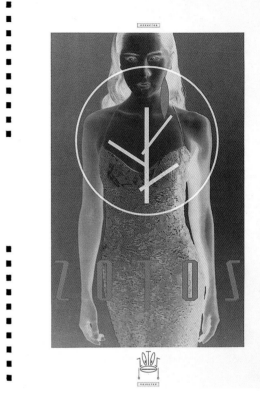

Rick Valicenti, *Esse, 1991.*

This promotion by Rick Valicenti of Thirst, Barrington, Illinois, for a new paper grade caused an uproar. Gilbert Paper addressed the issue of artistic expression in a letter to the design community that was tipped in to the promotion, stating that when a client selects a designer, the designer's "unique perspective is openly sought and actively heeded." Many disagreed and blasted Valicenti for his self-expressionistic assault, yet that didn't stop him. He continues to include personal art in his work, including a series of subsequent (and, possibly, even more inflammatory) Gilbert promotions.

Back to the Future

Like their early counterparts, today's Radical designers feel their profession is much more than the regimented **marketing tool** many claim it should be. Today's Radicals have come full circle in many ways, returning to the roots of design that were propagated in the early decades of the twentieth century when artists—such as FORTUNATO DEPERO, who incorporated Futurist philosophy into many of his posters, advertisements, and typographic creations, and KURT SCHWITTERS, whose collage compositions employed many Dada techniques—enthusiastically injected their designs with a personal artistic vein and **moral conscience**. Many of these early practitioners relied on the Cubists, Dadaists, Futurists, Surrealists, and other fine artists engaged in pushing the envelope for inspiration. **Exploration** was an important part of the process. PIET ZWART, for instance, searched for ways to combine the disciplines of *De Stijl*—a Dutch magazine and art movement begun by THÉO VAN DOESBURG in 1917 that sought abstract objectivity— with Dadaism's disdain for conventional techniques and turn them into one vital, reader-friendly design style. So while the **client's needs** were important, the **designer's voice** was an equally vital component. The two forces worked in harmony.

The **chaotic** social, political, cultural, and economic **climate** that existed in those early years is at least partially responsible for this visual revolution. A world war had been fought, and soon there were rumblings of another one on the horizon; many countries were suffering a financial depression. Yet sandwiched in between the massive pitfalls were bursts of great **progress**. Electricity was fast becoming a necessity rather than a luxury; automobiles, aircraft, and trains made it easy to move people and products across the world; technology was rapidly advancing; and as a result, industries were spreading their wings globally. In *A History of Graphic Design: 2nd Edition* (Van Nostrand Reinhold, New York, 1992), historian PHILIP MEGGS states:

> *"Against this turbulence, it is not surprising that visual art experienced a series of creative revolutions that questioned its values, approaches to organizing space, and role in society . . . . Elemental ideas about color and form, social protest, and the expression of Freudian theories and deeply personal emotional states occupied many artists."*

Such thinking was perpetuated by that sacred temple of aesthetics, the Bauhaus, which was founded in 1919 in Germany and where artists WASSILY KANDINSKY, PAUL KLEE, and PIET MONDRIAN taught alongside designers HERBERT BAYER and LÁSZLÓ MOHOLY-NAGY. The Bauhaus combined fine arts

Steff Geissbuhler, *Geigy brochure,* 1965.
This brochure by Steff Geissbuhler, now with Chermayeff Geismar, Inc., in New York, achieves a layered, almost three-dimensional vortex—an expansion of the International Style's parameters. Although it was done long before the computer appeared in design studios, the brochure looks like a digital work.

sensibilities with the more pragmatic dictums of Russian Constructivism, the revolutionary **abstract art** movement begun in 1917 that strove to incorporate **beauty** into modern **industrial materials** (such as glass and plastic). For a period of fourteen years, the Bauhaus school was an artistic greenhouse that attempted to fuse art, architecture, and design into a **unified whole**. Though short-lived (Nazi pressure caused the faculty to vote to dissolve it in August 1933), its influence had a virtual domino effect on art and design, one whose impact is still felt today. For example, the "Great Constructivist" EL LISSITZKY lectured there several times in the early 1920s, helping to bring the principles of the Constructivist movement to Berlin. He inspired artist KURT SCHWITTERS to explore Constructivist design and typography. Schwitters was taken by the creative potential of this exciting arena and thrust himself into it full force, founding the Ring Neue Werbegestalter (Circle of the New Advertising Typographer) of which ZWART and JAN TSCHICHOLD, among others, were members. In turn, the Bauhaus helped introduced Lissitzky to the concepts of De Stijl, Dadaism, and other artistic trains of thought; he eventually spread their theories back home in Russia. The **circle** rolled on.

Embarkation, education, imagination. More conundrums confront today's designers than ever. After mastering new software upgrades, peripherals, languages, CD-roms, megamemory, megapower (my bytes are bigger than yours!) the super information highway, etc., etc., there are typesetting, trapping, production from disk to output to tackle. (So who makes the coffee?) *Where's it all end?*

what?

The bigger question is, *where does it all begin?* Designers aiming to conquer this exciting frontier must not be afraid to embark upon a new journey of learning, nor be reticent about letting the machine become a part of their creative process — a freewheeling interaction of human emotion, imagination and digital dimensionality.

Luscious cherries atop the digital dessert.

■ ▨ *black and match yellow duotone*

5

"With all the technology at your command, yes—being able to fully customize your work or put your handwriting into blocks of text with full editing capabilities—computers do indeed allow for personal encoding. Computers do not make everything look alike. It's just that so many people tend to sit at the computer and do the same things."

PRODUCTION NOTES

This image printed 4-color process in 133-line screens with a match silver metallic and an overall matte varnish. The wood texture on top printed as a process quadtone with dominant cyan and magenta. The upper image was divided vertically. The left printed in 150-line screens and the right printed in 175-line screens. The 3-dimensional type was converted to a fake duotone and printed silver metallic and black. The type was created in Pixar Typestry.

Passport Gypsum, 90 lb. Text, Smooth Finish.

There is one huge difference between today's vanguard and those early avant-garde artists. The latter were engaged in a budding profession. While it certainly had its share of avid proponents of one style or another, its early artists were virtually unencumbered by expectations in comparison to the myriad **constraints** that have developed over time and which the Radicals now encounter. Today's Radicals also face another perplexing peril: becoming trite themselves. Each artistic revolution, at first loose and freeing, becomes codified into an aesthetic with rules and traditions. What is radical today can quickly become the standard. Tschichold is an example of this. He now is considered a stalwart of "traditional" design as one of the key developers (along with Lissitzky and Moholy-Nagy) of the New Typography movement, which developed in Europe in the 1920s and 1930s and which eventually became a major component of Modernism. New Typography advocated utilitarianism and simplicity through designs that featured **asymmetric** layouts created from **geometric** forms and **sans serif** typefaces. Yet, as the first to publicly spell out typographic standards for the profession in the insert he created for the October 1925 issue of *typographische mitteilungen* and in his 1928 book *Die Neue Typographie*, Tschichold became an unlikely yet major revolutionary of his day. Medieval-looking text and symmetrical layouts that had dominated German design for centuries still prevailed, so when Tschichold went public in advocating this radical new approach he created quite a stir. In fact, shortly after the book's publication he was arrested by the Nazis for his "un-German" creations and forced to emigrate to Switzerland.

If you look closely, you will see the process at work today: as the **mainstream shifts** to incorporate Radical work, Radical design is considered more mainstream. Its influence is creeping into all sorts of unlikely venues, from FRANKFURT BALKIND PARTNERS' award-winning annual report for Time-Warner to CARLOS SEGURA's MCI commercials and DAVID CARSON's Pepsi ads. The paradox for Radical designers is that their very success is making them less radical, so they must be ever-evolving. Continuous exploration is paramount to their survival.

Modern Radical Influences

As the name implies, Radical designers tend to draw their inspiration from innovative movements in art, politics, and culture at the extreme edge of society, and many trace their defining aesthetics to the turbulent 1960s. Certainly social and political issues in the 1960s, from war protests to women's rights and sexual freedom, served as fodder for many revolutionary design modes, and they are topics that are still timely today—along with AIDS awareness, the environment, and human rights.

But mainly the Radicals look to the artists and art movements of this era as their catalysts. Pop art, one example, grew out of the efforts of artists such as JASPER JOHNS, ROBERT RAUSCHENBERG, and ANDY WARHOL to make a statement on contemporary cultural values by creating fine art from mass-produced graphic ephemera. Designers didn't take long to reemploy and reappropriate this parody of their work, incorporating the art of the pop artists into their designs and further blurring the lines between art and commerce. Warhol's memorable Campbell's soup can painting, for instance, adorns not only museum walls but the food mogul's annual report.

Another even more intense countercultural expression was the psychedelic art scene that STEVEN HELLER, writing in *Print* (November/December 1989), said rejected the *"staid typographic and pictorial vocabulary of 'officialdom' for a universal sensory experience"* (an adventure often aided by mind-expanding drugs). Underground publications such as *Screw* magazine and *Zap Comix* also had a profound influence. *Zap* founder VICTOR MOSCOSO, who studied under former Bauhaus instructor JOSEF ALBERS, was a leader in both the psychedelia and underground comic movements. He said that the poster, the main vehicle for conveying the psychedelic style, worked because it was unencumbered by the rules of "good design." In a backlash against "establishment" attitudes, the posters typically employed colors that were meant to irritate and lettering that was intentionally hard to read. At the same time, underground comics used caustic images and loud lettering in chaotic arrangements to deal with taboo subjects. Today, such devices are often found in the work of RICK VALICENTI, CHARLES S. ANDERSON, and CARLOS SEGURA, among others.

There is also much common ground between Radical design today and the theories and art of the Fluxus movement, another revolutionary faction that grew out of the 1960s. Fluxus included designers, fine artists, and composers who believed in the unity of art and life, the overlapping of artistic disciplines—music and art, for example—globalism, exploration and research, random chance and

WHO IS THIS SLIMY CREATURE?

Raised by a single mom, but wants to put other fatherless children in orphanages.

Smoked pot in college, but seeks harsher penalties for drug use.

Dodged the draft, but plans to increase military spending.

Rants about government corruption, but agreed to a $4.5 million book advance/bribe from a company under investigation by Congress.

Divorced wife number one while she was in the hospital with cancer and is a deadbeat dad, but supports "traditional family values."

IT'S NEWT!

A PUBLIC SERVICE MESSAGE FROM **GUERRILLA GIRLS**

Guerrilla Girls, *It's Newt, 1995.*

Radical protesters tend to be even more caustic than their insurgent predecessors. This comment on Speaker of the House Newt Gingrich by the Guerrilla Girls, who describe themselves as "an anonymous band of masked avengers that fights racism and sexism in the art world," leaves no doubt about their feelings. Their protests appear in publications and on utility poles across the United States. This one ran in a 1995 issue (number 9) of Plazm *magazine, an experimental arts publication produced by designer Joshua Berger in Portland, Oregon.*

Charles S. Anderson, *Monster Candy,* 1989.
Monster comics of the 1960s influenced the work of Charles S. Anderson of Minneapolis, Minnesota, two decades later. His work for French Paper firmly established what became known as the retro look in the late 1980s and early 1990s.

playfulness, among other things. They often drew on aspects of Futurism, Dadaism, the 1920s Soviet group LEF (Left Front of the Arts), and Russian Constructivism. GEORGE MACIUNAS, who gave Fluxus its name and is considered the main creator of its printed works, was a primary leader, along with KEN FRIEDMAN, DICK HIGGINS, BEN VAUTIER, and MILAN KNIZAK. Maciunas's own academic background stands as an example of the Fluxus artists' crossover approach to art. He studied architecture, fine art, and graphic arts at the Cooper Union School of Art in New York before earning a degree in architecture from the Carnegie Institute of Technology in Pittsburgh in 1954. Print materials were the main vehicles used to promote the Fluxus cause, from posters and newspapers to catalogs and yearbooks. Budget limitations greatly affected the look of the pieces (a prime factor guiding much of today's Radical work). To economize, and because many designers appreciated its purity, a typewriter was often used to "set" copy. Maciunas suggested that another inexpensive way to develop typographic interest was to enlarge the text on a photocopier and to vary the letters' texture. As a result, Fluxus design often was reminiscent of early twentieth century broadsheets, employing a wide variety of headline typefaces, oversized letterforms for emphasis, angled copy, and inexpensive clip art.

The defining factor of the Fluxus artists was their hunger for exploration, a search for what works, according to Ken Friedman, who designed in the studios of both Maciunas and Dick Higgins. *"These were not careful experiments run by college teachers trying to get bumped up to professor, nor experiments designed to please a client,"* he commented in *Eye* (issue 7, 1992). *"These were challenging experiments, but no matter how adventurous and lively they seem today, they made no sense to people back in the 1960s."* Decades later, however, designers still applaud the work of the Fluxus artists for its stimulating freshness.

Fluxus also offers a prime example of artistic disciplinary crossbreeding. A major instigator of the Fluxus movement was composer JOHN CAGE, whose thinkings were disseminated by the artists who studied under him in the 1950s at the New School of Social Research in New York City. Cage, in turn, was ignited by the provocative Dadaist MARCEL DUCHAMP. Cage was drawn to Duchamp's attempts to *"put painting once again at the service of the mind . . . questioning every assumption about the boundaries of visual art,"* Calvin Tomkins wrote in the *New Yorker* (January 15, 1996). Inflammatory as the whole Dada movement was in its own right, Duchamp, especially, enraged many of his peers when he invented the "ready-made," poking fun at the concept of fine art by signing or assigning titles to common manufactured objects such as a urinal or a bicycle wheel mounted on a stool. Such thinking provided a perfect credo for the Fluxus artists' aberrant productions.

Music has always been a major force influencing design, particularly during the 1960s and early 1970s when it was one of the main vehicles for articulating the era's revolutionary messages. Commercial sales of music set unprecedented records, and designers were encouraged to concoct outrageous, lavish LP covers and inserts that were often as raucous and rebellious as the music. Many endure as revered pieces of art in their own right. The famous poster/record insert that MILTON GLASER created in 1967 featuring a psychedelic, rainbow-haired profile of Bob Dylan, and Spencer Drate's peelable banana cover for the Velvet Underground, which paid homage to Warhol's peelable cow and Coke bottle wallpaper, are two prime examples. Music has played an equally important role in shaping 1990s design, so much so that Carlos Segura advises his peers to view music stores as contemporary museums, where the latest in the profession's styles and techniques can be found.

European Mail-Order Warehouse/*Fluxshop,** *1965.*

The Fluxus artists' concern with economy—most of their projects were low-budget—led them to employ cheap, common typography and printing techniques. The resulting industrial, funky look of their work is seen in this recreation of a Fluxus workshop for a 1984 exhibit at the Contemporary Arts Museum in Houston.

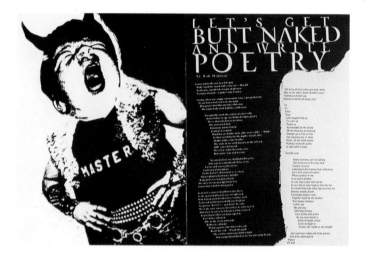

Smay Vision, *Let's Get Butt-Naked and Write Poetry,* 1996.

This spread designed by Smay Vision for Plazm combines concrete (or pattern) poetry with an in-your-face attitude and a strong sense of humor. The images were scanned from old magazines and the designers' vast junk collection.

If experiments and trends in the fine art and music worlds have left their mark on design, so too have literature and poetry. Some of the more interesting experiments have come from 1920s Dadaists such as KURT SCHWITTERS, who both wrote and designed poetry by separating the words from their language context and presenting them as visual components to be read as pure sounds. Four decades later in the 1960s, the concrete poets once again explored this avenue. In essence, they were all playing with an ancient writing form called pattern poetry in which the typographical arrangement of the text formed a visual design that also conveyed a message—although, unlike the Dadists and concrete poets, the pattern poets worked within a few standard forms and did not attempt to make each work unique. Design researcher HERB STRATFORD theorizes that such poets and the Radicals have many things in common. All were attempting to *"communicate on several levels simultaneously and challenge the traditional idea of the poem as a static description or arrangement of words. . . . [They] attempt to utilize text in a way that pushes the boundaries of accepted usage for their individual times and mediums,"* he said in his 1994 graduate thesis *"Word As Image: Concrete Poetry and Contemporary Communications."*

The heady literary movement of the BEATS likewise left its mark on design, both in the 1950s when it began and again on the Radicals forty years later. The Beats often incorporated the staccato rhythms of jazz into their writing. Noted poet ALLEN GINSBERG frequently used spacing or typestyle to emphasize certain words in his compositions in an attempt to guide the reader's emotion and the reciter's tempo. Designer SAUL BASS picked up on this and emulated the staccato pace of Elmer Bernstein's remarkable jazz score for the 1955 movie *The Man with the Golden Arm* by using jagged lines in its opening sequence and print graphics. Today, the Beat movement's rebellious leaders have become countercultural

"bill"

swag®

snowboarding apparel / 5651 palmer way, #j, carlsbad, ca 92008 / send $2 for stickers and info

Swag ad, *1994.*

Beat writers have inspired many of today's young Radicals. William Burroughs, who starred in this apparel ad for snowboarders in the July 1994 issue of blu r *magazine, is a favorite. (The ad has a possibly unintentional reference to when Burroughs killed his wife while attempting to shoot a glass off her head.)*

Spencer Drate, *The Velvet Underground CD*, 1993.

More than twenty years after disbanding, the legendary Velvet Underground held a reunion concert in Paris. Warner Bros. Records commissioned Spencer Drate, the New York–based designer of the original Velvet Underground LP covers, to create a commemorative package. Drate used elements from his memorable peelable banana cover of the late 1960s (a takeoff on Andy Warhol's peelable wallpaper) to create the limited-edition CD cover.

icons themselves for a new generation, and astute manufacturers of youth-related products have been fast to cash in on the popularity of Ginsberg, JACK KEROUAC, and WILLIAM BURROUGHS, among others, featuring them in Gap ads, Nike commercials, snowboard apparel ads, and other campaigns.

Still, perhaps, no literary or artistic movement has more in common with the Radicals than the New Journalists. The New Journalists emerged in the late 1950s and 1960s to become participatory chroniclers of their times. They included raucous spirits like HUNTER S. THOMPSON, who hopped on a Harley and roared down the highway alongside the Hell's Angels into gonzo glory, and adventurous intellectuals, such as GEORGE PLIMPTON, who stepped into the ring with boxing champion Archie Moore and took a pounding so he could truly comprehend the sport's brutal artistry. These talents resurrected the art of reporting, which had deteriorated through the years into mostly a cold, factual diatribe, by thumbing their noses at the sacred tradition of objectivity—much like the Radicals mock the standard precepts of "objective" design communication. The New Journalists recognized that certain types of stories called for a passionate stance, and they scaled the Great Wall between narrator and participant to become part of the experience. This permitted them to inject their stories with an emotionally articulated point of view. At first, the journalistic establishment villified these innovators, but today New Journalism is considered an important and effective part of the vernacular.

In the same manner, design's Radicals inject their work with emotion and a personal point of view. Then they go a step further—they also engage the viewers, so they are not simply objective observers but instead must interact with a communiqué to truly understand it. In doing so these designers, too, step over the boundary between narrator and participant to become the New Visualists of communication.

Jack CK Chen and Lou Dorfsman, *The Museum of Television & Radio,* 1996.
In the late 1990s, technology offered a new vehicle for designers—the World Wide Web. They quickly tapped into this new creative outlet, combining animation, sound, and print capabilities into a single expression. And for the first time they could instantly interact with millions of viewers. Many Web site designs are linked to the client's more traditional marketing program, as shown here in these works created by Chen (Web site) and Dorfsman (schedule concepts) for the Museum of Television and Radio in New York.

The Web and Beyond

Technological pundit NEIL POSTMAN once remarked: *"A new technology does not add or subtract something. It changes everything."*

That is especially true of the design profession. Technology has always played a huge part in design revolutions, from the printing press to movable type, the typewriter to phototypesetting. However, no one could have foreseen the unprecedented effect the personal computer would have. It has changed not only how designers design but how they work with vendors, how clients perceive them, and even how they operate their businesses and price their work.

It also has changed what designers design. Like a viral strain, technology is constantly mutating into new forms, from desktop publishing and the CD-ROM to the Internet and its World Wide Web. By the mid-1990s, hundreds of thousands of Web sites were up and running, but marketing analysts say they represent just the tip of the coming iceberg. Publication specialist turned Web master ROGER BLACK predicted that by the year 2010 the Web will have crept into all aspects of our lives, telling our ovens how hot to get in order to cook our dinners and directing our cars where to go when we're lost (*HOW* magazine, August 1998).

Designing a good Web site requires keen coding and programming skills (or teaming up with a technologist to handle these functions), along with a mastery of design, animation, and storyboarding, among other abilities. The look must be kinetic and compelling, and it must grab the viewer's attention in a split second. Computer consultant/designer MICHAEL SULLIVAN predicted in a February 1996 *HOW* magazine article that the next technological breakthroughs would come in the form of "hybrid media." He said these would result from the merger of multimedia and online publishing, and would include "smart media," which would use underlying databases to provide ubiquitous information displays.

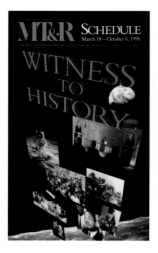

The Radicals' energetic styles and exploratory natures seem well suited to tackle the design challenges that are sure to arise from these and other new arenas.

Showing Radical Respect

Today's design Radicals defy stereotyping, running the gamut from CARLOS SEGURA, whose designs typically have a chaotic, ethereal quality, to DANA ARNETT, who prefers that a project's concept rather than its presentation be revolutionary. Yet they all have one thing in common that brands them as Radicals: they have set, and are setting, new standards for the profession. They are doing this through several shared traits, most notably through their quest for new and exciting ways to communicate with their audiences and through a general desire to upset established thinking, to incorporate subjectivity into their work, to include both social and political commentary, and to blur the line between fine art and commerce. As a result, they are often controversial.

On the following pages is a select group of designers whose work is Radical for one or more of these reasons and who, through their commitment to provoking convention, will likely continue to set standards. They include contemporary artists who have been among the greatest influences of the Radicals (found among Mentors) and the current crop of groundbreakers (Innovators). Finally, a group of artists who promise to be tomorrow's revolutionary leaders (Progeny) wraps up the profile sections. These categories are loosely organized, however—for instance, the *Emigre* artists are listed among Mentors, but could just as appropriately be placed in Innovators. In fact, unless they are deceased, most mentors are still going strong alongside the innovators. That, too, is a Radical trait.

While the people profiled in this book by no means represent a complete anthology of the Radicals (some prominent designers are missing here for a number of reasons), they are in the very forefront of this exhilarating journey. They and their adventuresome brethren represent the best of what the Radical movement is about.

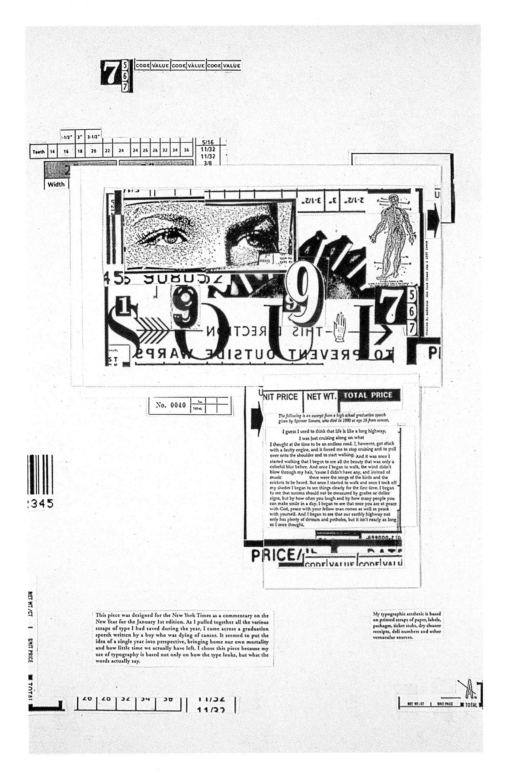

The following is an excerpt from a high school graduation speech given by Spenser Somers, who died in 1990 at age 18 from cancer.

I guess I used to think that life is like a long highway. I was just cruising along on what I thought at the time to be an endless road. I, however, got stuck with a faulty engine, and it forced me to stop cruising and to pull over onto the shoulder and to start walking. And it was once I started walking that I began to see all the beauty that was only a colorful blur before. And once I began to walk, the wind didn't blow through my hair, 'cause I didn't have any, and instead of music there were the songs of the birds and the crickets to be heard. But once I started to walk and once I took off my shades I began to see things clearly for the first time. I began to see that success should not be measured by grades or dollar signs, but by how often you laugh and by how many people you can make smile in a day. I began to see that once you are at peace with God, peace with your fellow man comes as well as peace with yourself. And I began to see that our earthly highway not only has plenty of detours and potholes, but it isn't nearly as long as I once thought.

This piece was designed for the New York Times as a commentary on the New Year for the January 1st edition. As I pulled together all the various scraps of type I had saved during the year, I came across a graduation speech written by a boy who was dying of cancer. It seemed to put the idea of a single year into perspective, bringing home our own mortality and how little time we actually have left. I chose this piece because my use of typography is based not only on how the type looks, but what the words actually say.

My typographic aesthetic is based on printed scraps of paper, labels, packages, ticket stubs, dry cleaner receipts, deli numbers and other vernacular sources.

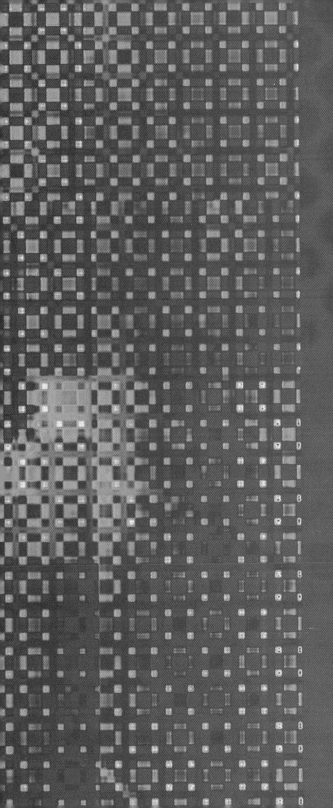

mentors

pierre bernard

Atelier de Création Graphique, Paris, France

iconoclastic complicity

In May 1968, Paris was brought to a standstill by widespread antigovernment rioting sparked by student protests. These events helped define PIERRE BERNARD'S graphics mission for years to come. Bernard collaborated with fellow designers FRANCOIS MIEHE and GERARD PARIS-CLAVEL—whom he had met in school at the Ecole Supérieure des Arts Décoratifs (National School of Decorative Arts) in Paris—to produce subversive posters that peppered the streets during those tumultuous days. Shortly thereafter, the trio decided to join forces professionally.

They called their studio Grapus, merging the word *graphique* with *crapules staliniennes,* which translates to "Stalinist scum," a term reserved at the time for France's left-wing radicals. The name reflects the mind-set of the designers and the ideals that drove them for the next two decades. They vowed not to let commercial work become the primary impetus of their professional practice, in the long-standing tradition of avant-garde artists such as LESTER BEALL, whose memorable *Germany Yesterday—Germany Tomorrow* broadside poster, designed in 1939 for the New York World's Fair's Freedom Pavilion (which was never built), warned the world about the Nazis. Instead, they would use their talent to fight the abundance of injustices existing worldwide. Apartheid and nuclear weapons were just two of the social, cultural, and political diseases they sought to cure through doses of graphic conscience. Over the next two decades, Grapus provided an ethical voice for the design community, one whose messages echoed loudly and clearly around the globe.

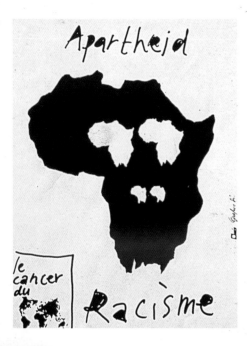

Apartheid, Racism, 1986.

Grapus disbanded in 1991 and its partners formed their own separate practices, carrying with them the original spirit. Even today, Bernard feels that his studio's work (which he operates with partner DIRK BEHAGE) is a series of opportunities that allow them to evaluate social exchanges in a cultural context. He takes on only those projects related to what he considers *"enthusiastic human activities,"* that is, those activities his designers can appreciate and, most importantly, feel passionate about.

Bernard's work is characterized by his uncanny ability to convey complex messages in an uncluttered manner that cuts straight to the crux of the assignment. He often places common icons and words in situations that lend them an entirely new context. The African continent, for instance, is a looming black skull in his powerful and prophetic poster protesting apartheid in South Africa. A nipple-topped Coca-Cola

Gevrey-Chambertin, *1982.*

This poster does double duty, as a promotion for a play and
as a protest against Corporate America's infiltration of the world.
It demonstrates Grapus's strong stands against injustice.

Decide Tomorrow Today, *1991.*

This poster was created for an Atelier de Création Graphique/Grapus
exhibition at the Orleans Institute of Visual Arts.

Louvre identity system, *1989.*

Among Grapus's best-known projects is its identity system for the Louvre. This poster offers a contemporary view of a two-hundred-year-old Giovanni Paolo Pannini painting, using digital technology to compress the artist's eighteenth-century work. The poster was intended to acknowledge the Louvre project's donors.

Design Renaissance, *1993.*
Bernard designed this compelling poster to announce the Icograda conference in Glasgow. The smudges represent "getting one's hands into the axle grease," conveying the design ideal of artists becoming totally immersed in their creative process.

bottle relays a courageous stand against Corporate America's corruption of culture in a poster promoting a play named for a popular burgundy wine, Gevrey-Chambertin.

The artist's iconoclastic attitude does not mean he discounts clients' views; on the contrary, he chooses his clients with the utmost care. *"The fit between designer and client requires trust— better still, complicity,"* he remarks. *"From this is born a quality relationship with the audience, which will be invited, little by little, to share in [the complicity]."* Bernard's work has had a large impact on the design profession, not merely because of his desire to make a radical political statement, but because of the experience and research he brings to each project. He has a fine-tuned sensibility for how to exploit the inherent uniqueness of each piece in its proper design category, whether poster, catalog, or magazine cover.

Bernard attended the Ecole Supérieure des Arts Décoratifs during the early 1960s, which, in his opinion, marked the beginning of general instruction in graphic design. Later he studied in Warsaw at the Academy of Arts, under master poster artist HENRYK TOMASZEWSKI. Posters were and still are Bernard's trademark; it is through them that he best voices his views. His work reflects the experience of the Paris insurrection and his twenty years at Grapus—the revolt because it instilled in him a sense of purpose, and Grapus because of the partners' intense bond, which gave them confidence to fearlessly *"promote Utopia as the principal realistic value."*

Perhaps Bernard's greatest motivation, however, is Tomaszewski, whose acerbic wit and simple, potent style have influenced generations. Bernard credits those years studying in Poland for his heightened sense of *"plastic and poetic sensibility."* Tomaszewski, in particular, instilled in him the conviction that only through using his own artistic sensibility could he produce something of true value, something intriguing enough to offer the world.

National Parks identity system, 1990–97.

The French government has hired Bernard, despite his reputation as a "subversive," to create some of its most visible icons, such as this logo for the country's national parks system. The logo's applications are wide ranging, from signage and literature to rangers' badges. Looking closely, one can identify the flora and fauna that make up the emblem's swirl.

neville brody

Research Studios, London, England

the pathfinder

In the early 1980s, NEVILLE BRODY made design history with his introduction of the new look for *The Face,* a British style magazine for which he was the art director. Bit by bit, over the course of several issues, he deconstructed magazine elements such as the banner, section logos, and standing headlines and then just as slowly, issue by issue, rebuilt them into abstract marks. Brody says he was investigating the process of visual coding and its role in the editorial environment. The public was intrigued, and they snapped up copies of *The Face* as much to witness its visual metamorphosis as to peruse its articles.

That project and other equally inventive visual contrivances were brought to the global design community's attention with the 1988 publication of his book *The Graphic Language of Neville Brody* (cowritten with Jon Wozencraft, Rizzoli), whose release coincided with the exhibition of a ten-year retrospective of Brody's work at Britain's Victoria and Albert Museum. In effect, the book served as a clip art collection of ideas and work samples that were quickly plagiarized by every level of designer, from student to major advertising agency art director. Brody fast became one of the most mimicked designers of the late twentieth century.

Considering this, the instructors who flunked Brody out of design school because they found his work "uncommercial" probably would prefer to remain anonymous. Brody, a native of Southgate, a northern London suburb, began his academic training in 1975 as a fine arts student at Hornsey College of Art. He soon switched to design because he found his initial choice "too elitist." Much like his idol ALEXANDER RODCHENKO, the Russian Constructivist of the 1920s who abandoned pure art in favor of visual communication that served society's needs, Brody believed in art for the masses. He reasoned that design school would pro-

8 Eyed Spy, Diddy Wah Diddy, 1982.

This LP sleeve for a garage-music band that recorded on the Fetish label was created shortly after Brody left design school, while he was living in a squat in Covent Garden and washing dishes in a restaurant to help get by. The emotional masklike image on the sleeve's cover and the grotesque skeletal form on the back inject the work with a human expressiveness that Brody found lacking in much design of that time.

The Face contents pages, Nos. 50–55, *1984.*

Achieving a modular design based on the idea of a set of units that fit together according to their use, plus a quest for a more organic design that changed over a period of time drove Brody to metamorphose The Face's *contents page logo over the course of several issues to communicate not by word but by iconography.*

vide the perfect venue for his investigation into what sort of artistic endeavors might attract the interest of viewers from all walks of life. So he entered the three-year course in graphic design offered by the London College of Printing (LCP).

Much to his disappointment, Brody found LCP "restrictive and pedestrian," while, ironically, his instructors felt his work was beyond the comprehension of a general audience. After one year of graphic arts training he'd had enough, and he left to try his hand in the professional design world. It was 1979 and the height of Britain's punk rock movement, which conveyed a dismal message of industrial and social decay. This intensified Brody's conviction that the commercial market treated the human element in a cold, plastic manner. He wanted to take a painterly, artistic design approach, much like that seen in the photographs of MAN RAY and LÁSZLÓ MOHOLY-NAGY, to help reintroduce emotion into design. Not only did the music world stimulate Brody's thought and design processes, but it offered him a job his first year out of school as a designer of album covers at a small record label called *Rocking Russian*. He soon moved on to a similar position for *Stint*. He spent a total of two years at *Rocking Russian* and *Stint* before joining the independent label *Fetish* in 1981, where he felt truly free to follow his own impulses. His cover work for releases by such bands as Clock, 8 Eyed Spy, and 23 Skidoo was consumed by primitive, almost tribal symbolism and markings that evoked strong emotion—conveyed through ritualistic paintings, clay sculptures, and macabre shapes, all vividly reproduced in the two-color printing process.

That same year, Brody also became art director and designer at the British men's lifestyle magazine *The Face,* where he soon turned his attention from imagery to typography. Brody believed that most type in the early 1980s was *"boring and overladen with traditions that repelled change,"* and he sought to force excitement into it by combining unrelated fonts, arranging the letters or words in unusual configurations, or manipulating them on the photocopier into illegible shapes and proportions. Eventually, he progressed to drawing his own faces and

Arena, *Winter,* *1986.*

Brody's early work for the men's lifestyle magazine Arena *(shown is an opening page for its Avanti section) demonstrates a shift from the expressive visual mode he employed as art director of* The Face *to a minimalistic, non-decorative typographic style.*

Interview *magazine page,* 1994.

developed a series of geometric sans serif letters that gave the magazine a completely distinct look.

Five years later and ready for a new design tack, Brody moved on to *Arena,* a rival style magazine. It was high time, he decided, to *"take some of the hysteria out of contemporary design"* and put the emphasis back on content. His hand-drawn logo and refined template for *Arena* relied heavily on emotive photography, contrasted by text set in bland Helvetica Black. This was an abrupt about-face from his previous work. In later issues, Brody returned to expressive, painterly typography such as that seen in *The Face,* but unlike the hip attitude of that publication, *Arena* always exuded quiet elegance. Brody hoped that this totally different approach might put a halt to those who favored his *Face* work and so eagerly imitated it. But his quest for individuality backfired. *Arena'*s look was much easier to copy than *The Face'*s, and once again Brody's influence proliferated throughout the design scene.

Eager to get out of the public spotlight, Brody retreated to his own studio, where he vowed to maintain a lower profile than that offered by the commercial and public arena of record labels and magazines. He now works for visually progressive clients such as Nike, Micromedia, and the Japanese clothier Men's Bigi. Rather than operate under his own name, Brody calls his firm, simply, Research Studios. This allows the other designers who work with him a chance to establish themselves free of his shadow. The name also indicates the spirit of Brody's work—experimental design. The only questions that must be answered before Research Studios accepts a project, Brody says, are whether it is challenging and whether it might lead to new creative territories. The designers at Research Studios concentrate on exploring new media, probing their structures and gestures. Books, packaging, Web sites, television graphics (he and two partners formed an Austria-German company called DMC to develop television design systems), and experimental CD-ROMs (working closely with Digitalogue in Japan) are just a few of the areas in which Research Studios delves. A series of one-man exhibitions and a partnership with ERIK SPIEKERMANN in the typography house FontShop International also consume Brody's calendar.

Fuse 11 & 15 posters, *1995–96.*

Fuse is an experimental typography publication Brody produces in conjunction with FontShop International (of which he is a director). Brody created these posters to promote his typeface contributions for the eleventh and fifteenth issues.

Perhaps, however, the most vital experiment to come from Research Studios is *Fuse,* a purely no-holds-barred typographic design publication featuring the work of some of today's most innovative artists. *"[Designer] Jeffery Keedy described it best,"* Brody notes of the magazine's premise, *"when he said that the abstract form has been explored and encouraged in painting, literature, and music, but never in design. Fuse is a liberation from that, a creative forum of abstract typography that opens up the perception of what typographic language is all about."* There's no doubt that Brody could have chosen to sit back and reap the benefits of an outstanding career, but that is the antithesis of everything he is about. *"Communication should not be allowed to become stagnant; ideas should never stop,"* he says. *"Language should be a continual organic type of evolution."* Designers should never become comfortable with designing in the same manner or resorting to design trends. As soon as that happens, Brody cautions, *"Your work ceases to have the power to change things."*

art chantry

Art Chantry Studio, Seattle, Washington

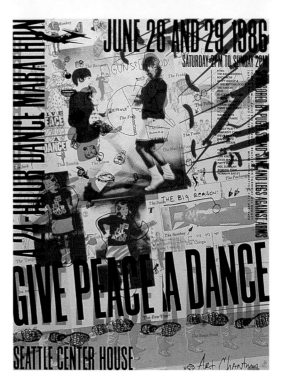

Give Peace a Dance, 1986.

Most of Chantry's work is very low budget, created for public service or arts organizations.

don't tread on me

ART CHANTRY feels his designs are better labeled "reactionary" rather than Radical. Each piece is a response to his environs and speaks accordingly. A close study of his work reveals a classic design approach; it's the imagery, elicited from the designer's own experience and cultural environment, that makes it appear extreme.

However, Chantry admits that the term "radical" does accurately describe his attitude. He dismisses all elitism and didactic posturing with such compulsion that his graphic design ideas, he says, are forever *"polluted"* by his bigotry toward the *"arrogant establishment"* order. *"All popular culture exists in denial of the rules and I live in a pop culture,"* he remarks. *"Whatever you tell me can or can't be done, I do the opposite. The results may appear 'radical' in a low-definition form, but are actually reactionary on a political spectrum."* He goes for the shock value, a trait soundly demonstrated in the promotional poster he created for musician MIKE JOHNSON. Rather than feature an image of the musician himself, Chantry snatches viewers' attention by using the frightening countenance of one of the twentieth century's most maniacal criminals—CHARLES MANSON.

Chantry's iconoclastic work and attitude are by-products of growing up impoverished. To escape, he turned to pop culture. Comic books, psychedelic posters, record covers, monster magazines, and television provided welcome relief. How these elements of his past bear on his work today is seen in Chantry's bold, sometimes even crude color sense; his love for cultural iconography; the close relationship he creates in his work between type and image; and his juxtapositioning of seemingly contradictory ideas to create whole new sensibilities.

Chantry's curiosity compels him to continually explore unfamiliar terrain, philosophies, and ideas. His first career choice was archaeology, and in a way, Chantry believes he has come full circle. He is a pop culture archaeologist who probes artifacts that are of his own and his peers' making. *"Design culture has no more immediacy for me than surfer culture or Babylonian culture,"* he comments. *"It's all part of a much larger whole. Most designers never seem to think*

The Holidays, 1995.

Mike Johnson: Built to Spill, 1995.

Cheater Slicks Mono Men, *1996.*

Chantry's work often dismantles sacred icons, as shown is his irreverent take-off on the acclaimed Saul Bass poster for The Man with the Golden Arm.

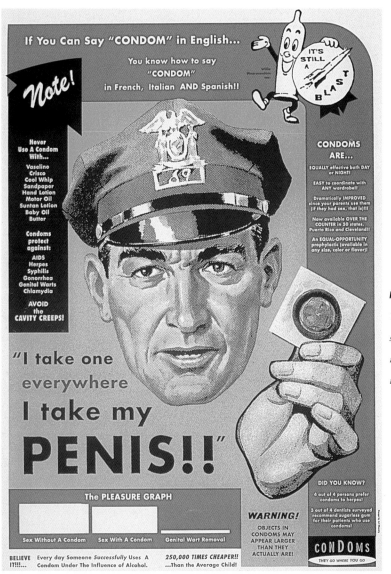

I Take My Penis, *1996.*

The design vernacular of the 1950s is resurrected in this humorous public service announcement. The choice of imagery not only serves as a very important reminder for its audience but also lampoons the retro movement that was ubiquitous in design during the late 1980s and 1990s.

Boycott Quarterly, *1997.*

about these things and quit at making a project look attractive for a client. That's decoration, not design."

Another vital factor in defining Chantry's visual persona is his lack of a formal design education. It took him six years to earn a bachelor's degree, as he kept getting sidetracked by classes that did not count toward his degree. Philosophy, in particular, fascinated him, as it explores the way knowledge interlocks. *"I saw the whole forest by taking philosophy classes, then I proceeded to learn about as many trees as I could,"* he notes. Chantry eventually earned a degree in painting, simply because he had accrued enough hours in that area. Still, he has great respect for the work of several design masters, particularly those who have operated out of the spotlight—HARRY CHESTER, ROBERT BROWNJOHN, TERRY GILLIAM, CAL SCHENKEL, and NORMAN LALIBERTE among them. Chantry admires them more for their conceptual ability than their execution skills. Ideas drive design, he believes; high production values are meaningless.

His rebellious nature aside, Chantry is profoundly directed by his clientele on every project. He works closely with clients to discern their thoughts, philosophies, and moods and to understand the audiences they want to reach. *"To do the job properly, the designer to some extent becomes the client,"* Chantry says. *"The result is more of a counseling or therapy process than [what most clients assume] is a product purchase."*

Though he once pursued corporate and advertising work, Chantry was never able to develop a satisfying relationship with those types of clients. Eventually, he tired of the game and gave up working for money to concentrate on the kinds of projects that he loves. Today, he just follows his interests; mostly they result in very low-budget posters. There are days, however, when Chantry experiences the urge once again to go after corporate clients; this time, however, a vengeful kind of enlightenment would be his goal. *"I'd buy an Armani suit and talk the talk, walk the walk, and suck as much money out of them as I could,"* he says. *"But I'd leave behind a ticking bomb in the form of graphic design, with too many layers of meaning for them to grasp. I've seen it done before, and it can destroy the enemy."*

spencer drate
jütka salavetz

Just Design, New York, New York

rockin' and rollin' along

The turbulent rock 'n' roll arena in which SPENCER DRATE and JÜTKA SALAVETZ operate not only keeps their work prominent among their peers but puts it squarely in the public eye. They count among those few designers whose accomplishments have been featured on MTV and VH1 as well as in the *New York Times* and *Smithsonian*. Their visual concoctions lithely traverse generations with winning appeal. In 1979, five years before Salavetz joined him, Drate was nominated for a coveted Grammy, along with codesigners DAVID BYRNE and JERRY HARRISON, for the Talking Heads' *Fear of Music* LP package. In 1993, Drate and Salavetz's special metal-box edition of LOU REED's *Magic and Loss* became a collectible even before the CD's formal release.

The youthful, energetic vibrations of the music industry help the pair's work remain as fresh and lively today as when Drate was literally plucked off the streets in the early 1970s to begin designing for rock stars. He was out for a stroll in New York City one afternoon when he bumped into a friend with whom he used to run underground movies during their days at the University of Bridgeport. The friend was designing ads for JOHN LENNON's *Imagine* album and needed help. So Drate accepted. That chance meeting set him on the road to a long and successful career in music graphics, working with clients like Sire Records, Warner Bros. Records, Sony Music, Polygram, and WCBS FM 101.1.

Drate's solo work in the 1970s often bordered on the psychedelic, inspired mostly by the personality of each artist client and funded by generous budgets that permitted the use of lavish materials. His radicalism was manifested mostly through the technical processes he employed. Day-Glo inks, complicated embosses, intricate die-cuts, and even peelable Colorform™-type images on Mylar were just a few of the visual tricks hiding up the designer's artistic sleeve. Then, as now, he acknowledges only one rule: total conceptual carry-through. Continuity is ensured by careful selection of typography, materials, and imagery. The idea must flow both literally and figuratively for the design to succeed.

Talking Heads, **Fear of Music,** *1979.*

Victory, *1981.*

Geoffrey Thomas's Helmut Newton-esque photograph was Drate's inspiration for this German band's LP cover. Four-color black-and-white process pumps up the photo.

Lou Reed, Magic and Loss, *1992.*

Sylvia Reed, Lou Reed's wife, was manager of the Velvet Underground and a designer. When she wanted to adapt cover art to a limited-edition CD, Drate, Salavetz, and Dennis Ascienzo assisted. Ascienzo scanned the art on a flatbed, then roughed up the edges in Adobe Photoshop. Next, he added "defects" by hand for a rustic, burned-out feel. He and Drate designed the inside paper liners together to maintain the visual flow. The CD label was scanned from granite-textured paper and colored in Adobe Photoshop. Ascienzo once again "burned away" the CD, cutting straight through all five color layers to the disk.

Then, virtually overnight, the music world changed. The generous LP budgets disappeared—as did the LPs themselves—with the advent of CDs in the mid-1980s. Music lovers applauded the superior sound, but designers were left puzzling over how to make the pared-down jewel box graphically appealing. However, Drate and Salavetz, who had joined Drate in 1984, were not among them.

Limited-edition and promotional CDs represented a whole new challenge, a chance to create something original. In their hands, the tiny jewel covers have become creative canvases of gigantic proportions. Drate and Salavetz's campaign to highlight the importance of this packaging area culminated in 1995 with the first *CD Special Packaging Exhibition*, which they conceived and curated for the One Club in New York. The exhibition featured over one hundred special CD packages, some of which were Grammy winners or nominees. True to the designers' longevity, several pieces chosen for the show were Drate and Salavetz's own handiwork. In 1997, their selected CD work was also exhibited in the Cooper-Hewitt National Museum of Design's *Mixed Messages* show.

Today, they have also crossed over into book packaging, stock agencies, CD-ROMs, software packaging, and corporate design. These sorts of clients can be diametrically opposed in attitude to the creatives operating within the music world, but that doesn't bother Drate and Salavetz. No matter who the client or what the project, the two continue to demonstrate their philosophy that creativity and imagination know no bounds.

Talking Heads, Cities, *1979.*

This LP sleeve featured abstract artwork by Plastics that

was chosen as a counterplay to the Talking Heads' music.

The Velvet Underground, Live MCMXCIII poster, *1993.*

Drate, Salavetz, and Ascienzo created this point-of-purchase poster for a special-edition

Velvet Underground CD set by continuing the banana theme. The CD cover itself, which

they also created, features a Colorform banana lift-off, in reference to an image on an earlier

Velvet Underground album that Drate had designed in the 1970s. The poster was chosen as

best of the year by Billboard *magazine in 1994.*

New York Gold, Volume 10, *1997.*

A contemporary takeoff on Piet Mondrian helps celebrate

the tenth anniversary of this photographers' showcase

and achieves the client's directive to create a "very hip

New York image."

zuzana licko
rudy vanderlans

Emigre, Sacramento, California

altering perception

Emigre partners ZUZANA LICKO and RUDY VANDERLANS's significant contribution to both the Radical cause and the entire communications process is threefold. First, there is Licko's pioneering exploration into digital typography. As one of a handful of designers in the mid-1980s who fully appreciated the creative potential of the computer's inherent bitmapped peculiarities, she exploited these characteristics in a series of progressively inventive fonts, in effect altering the design world's perception of computer typography. Second, there are the designs VanderLans fashions in *Emigre* magazine to show off his wife/partner's groundbreaking work, layouts largely derived from the computer fonts Licko creates. Since the two are often their own client, their work is an unadulterated expression of their ideas and ideologies.

Finally, there is the content of *Emigre* magazine itself. Licko and VanderLans initially envisioned *Emigre* as a fast method to disseminate their work. However, the magazine quickly rose to prominence as a showcase for the talents of many significant and like-minded artists. It also provided an international forum for scrutinizing new and experimental graphic design, focusing on design philosophy and the impact of visual communication on society. As the magazine has evolved through the years, it has become less of a showcase for design work and more of a forum for communication issues. Significantly, its readership now includes a number of sociologists and media watchers. VanderLans's designs have likewise changed to match the content, varying widely from a classically type-driven, grid-proper layout in one issue to a wildly distorted montage of imagery and typography in the next.

Still, the work always relies heavily on traditional design sensibilities, as a direct outcome of, or a response to, those sensibilities. VanderLans and Licko's ability to slip back and forth between the Radical and the classic is a direct result of their backgrounds. Licko is a native of Czechoslovakia and she received a BA in visual

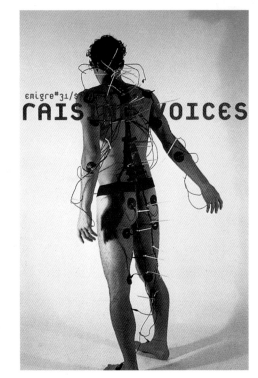

Raising Voices, *1994.*

The provocative cover imagery for Emigre *#31 is matched by an equally stimulating theme: the responsibility of education to design. The subject is typical of the magazine's theory-driven and critical approach, which is as much a part of its success as the courageous designs and typefaces found within its pages.*

Emigre #32, *1994.*

This seemingly conservative spread actually breaks many publishing layout strictures. The columns are clearly defined by rules, but the placement of text and line justifications within them vary from column to column to the point of sometimes butting into the rules. Fonts and text sizes vary within the same article in places, going down to a minuscule four points. Since headline and body text are similar, one must actually read the page to discover that a new article begins on the right.

Emigre #34, *1995.*

The issue prior to this one debuted Emigre's *new format, a more conservative 11½-by-8¼-inch size as opposed to the magazine's original 16¾ by 11¼ inches. The editorial focus shifted as well, from interviewing and displaying the work of individual designers to examining design and how it affects society. The change cost* Emigre *a number of subscriptions from the design sector, but it won many new readers from the sociology and communications fields.*

Emigre®

Sacramento, CA

1997 CATALOG

Emigre catalogs, fall 1996 and 1997.

Emigre *is not afraid to defy the wisdom of marketing experts even when selling its own products, witnessed in this series of catalogs that have no defining or linking format from one to the next.*

1996 Emigre Catalog
This free catalog contains over 150 typeface designs available for use on Mac and PC plus information on Emigre magazine, selected books on design, posters, Emigre music, postcards and more

Emigre #39, *1996.*

"Graphic Design and the Next Big Thing" is the subject of this enlightening issue.
VanderLans's design uses nothing but text on the cover and throughout, simply,
he explained, because no one knows what the next big thing involves.
"What I do know," he wrote in his preface, "is that in the near future, linear
reading and traditional publishing will experience serious competition from
electronic media. . . . It seemed fitting, then, that this issue would function also
as a tribute of sorts to a form of reading that is in serious jeopardy."

That was then, and this is now: but what is next?

By Lorraine Wild

The following essay is based on the transcript of a talk that I gave at *101: The Future of Design Education in the Context of Computer-Based Media,* a symposium organized by Louise Sandhaus and presented at the Jan van Eyck Akademie in Maastricht, The Netherlands, in November of 1995. It is highly speculative, and reading it now, I think that some of the conditions that I describe have already shifted, but that is the nature of the speed of change that confronts us. I was simply trying to capture and describe the moment that we educators and practitioners are in right now. (You blink, and it has changed.) I wish to thank the Jan van Eyck Akademie for giving me the assignment and the time to collect and record my thoughts.

I'm standing here not as an authority on multimedia or design education, but from the position of working inside of design education for twelve years, and connecting it with my own experience as a student from the mid-70s through the early 80s. That, and the context of my experiences at Cal Arts, and my ongoing experiences as a design practitioner in Los Angeles, have had an impact on the way that I see the future of work in design. I can't pretend that what I say will apply to all graphic design educators and practitioners everywhere. But in the U.S., Los Angeles is usually regarded as the place where both good and bad things happen first, because Californians are crazy and will try anything. Yet, usually, what happens there ends up happening everywhere else, sooner or later. So today I'm just speaking from my own experiences, but on the other hand, all I can say is: you'd better watch out I'd like to start by describing some recent observations that have affected my thoughts about what's going on in the profession that we are educating designers to enter.

The bigger picture

Recently the **Los Angeles Times** featured an article about one of the many invisible wars of rivalry between the metropolitan areas of San Francisco and Los Angeles, over which one would achieve economic domination in the new field of multimedia.[1] The gist of the article was that northern California held the lead in hardware (as in technology) development and financing, and that southern California held the lead in software (as in content) and its financing, and that it was not clear which area would end up drawing the most benefit from the phenomenal growth attached to the new technologies. But what caught my eye was that the state tax rolls already

1. *Multimedia is a new L.A.-S.F. Grudge Match; Will the Recently Matched Industry Next in Northern or Southern California?* by Amy Harmon. *L.A.Times,* 10/1/94, p.A-1 and *Hollywood and Technology; Welcome to Siliwood; Will the Convergence of the Creative and Technical Lead to a Jobs Revolution?* by Amy Harmon, *L.A.Times,* 9/12/95, p.J-4.

18
WILD

communication from the University of California, Berkeley, in 1984. VanderLans was born in The Hague and received a BA in graphic design from the Dutch Royal Academy of Fine Arts in 1979. He worked as a designer in the Netherlands before traveling to Berkeley to study photography in 1982, founding *Emigre* that same year along with a screenwriter and a poet, who subsequently moved on. Three issues later, Licko joined him and their acclaimed pioneering relationship took off.

The only thing separating design's innovators from its followers, they believe, is laziness, a trait no one could ever accuse them of possessing. Not only does their studio produce *Emigre* magazine, but it designs, manufactures, markets, and distributes Licko's fonts as well as exclusively licensed fonts from nearly twenty international designers, including Ed Fella and Bob Aufuldish.

Through the years the Emigre partners have endured their share of criticism from the design community for their inquisitive attitude and creations, but they don't let it sway them. Sometimes, they believe, a little controversy can be a good thing—it can even give work a greater significance. *"No matter what you do, some things are always misunderstood by some people,"* VanderLans explains. *"It is the very nature of communication, verbal or visual, to deny a single interpretation. It's what drives many designers crazy, but it's also what allows them to occasionally get away with murder. If innovative work is misunderstood at times, in the sense that people don't always get it, there are probably also times when it's been granted more meaning than was put in it."*

ed fella

California Institute of the Arts, Valencia, California

the anti·aesthetic aesthetic

During the thirty years ED FELLA spent as a commercial artist working for Detroit's top advertising agencies, he produced sophisticated illustrations and layouts, mainly for conservative automotive and healthcare clients. Such work concealed his subversive nature. Hidden behind a veil of Helvetica text, large, clean photographs, and rigidly structured columns lay a darker design side, one that earned Fella a consequential spot in *Emigre* magazine's "Wiseguys" issue (number 17, 1991).

Fella's seditious work would eventually come to have a great influence on young designers everywhere, starting with those in nearby Cranbrook Academy's acclaimed design program. Fella occasionally shared with the students in KATHERINE and MICHAEL MCCOY's classes the personally driven graphic media he created just for fun and his work for organizations in Detroit's thriving alternative art scene. Part of Fella's design appeal grew from his insistence on getting personal with his freelance design projects by injecting some of himself into them whenever possible. The catalog he produced in 1987 for a Detroit Focus Gallery exhibition of work by artists PHILLIP FIKE and BILL RAUHAUSER is a good example. Fella embellished portraits of the two artists, which appear on the catalog's center spread, with his own disconnected illustrative doodles. There's no apparent reason for having done so, beyond adding an interesting visual sideline. Yet a closer look reveals that his illustrations help hide the inferior quality of the two artists' photographs.

The Cranbrook students were also intrigued by how, using a direct-positive photostat machine (these were the precomputer days of the late seventies and early eighties), Fella fashioned collages from found imagery and bits and pieces of type, juxtaposing them in a manner that writer and designer LORRAINE WILD later described as *"a caricature of the minimalism of late Swiss corporate design"* (*Looking Closer 2: Critical Writings on Graphic Design,* Allworth Press, 1997).

New Writing series schedule, 1985.

Fella's inventive designs (much of it done for Detroit's alternative art scene) ultimately became a major influence for many designers. His impact can be seen by comparing this schedule, which he created for the Detroit Institute of Art, with Katherine McCoy's design five years later of the book Cranbrook Design: The New Discourse. *McCoy credits Fella for inspiring her own explorations and for helping shape Cranbrook's design program while she and her husband, Michael, served as cochairs.*

Detroit artists' market catalog, *1987.*

This piece cleverly announces two artists' work in a four-page format by showcasing metalsmith Phillip Fike on the opening spread and devoting the final spread to photographer Bill Rauhauser. Fella then creates a meeting of the two in the center. The catalog is remarkable for Fella's embellishment of the photographs with disconnected shapes.

Hard Werken lecture, AIGA Detroit, *1987.*

Fella's commercial illustrator side collides with his irreverent side in this engaging handbill promoting a lecture by the revolutionary Dutch design firm Hard Werken. Using the photocopier as his main tool, Fella created an entire aesthetic from bond paper, black ink, and an absence of halftones.

Holiday card, 1990.

Rules Are Taught, 1997.

Fella learned sign lettering at the trade school he attended while a high school student, an art that he perfected in the thirty years he spent as a commercial artist. Ever since graduating from Cranbrook, he's playfully loosened up the formal rigors of typography and of design in general. Fella's sentiments are appropriately expressed in a poster announcing his lecture.

The McCoys, who were in the process of establishing Cranbrook's program, greatly admired Fella's work and intellect, and they used his art and ideas as guideposts. Fella himself soon numbered among their students. At age forty-eight, he enrolled in the school's graduate program to supplement the design education that he had gained when he attended technical trade school during his high school years. The instructors there were from the New Bauhaus in Chicago. Expanding upon their ideas and attitudes, Cranbrook offered a creative environment free from constraints and encouraged the constant exploration and questioning of all that was inherent to design. Fella was more than just a student, however; he was a mentor to his classmates and his instructors, a driving force behind Cranbrook's analytical attitude. The Cranbrook experience forever changed both him and those with whom he came in contact.

After graduating from Cranbrook, Fella abandoned the commercial world for the academic, accepting a teaching post at the California Institute of the Arts (CalArts) where he still works today. Academia allows him to continue his design experiments without the rigors of a business-imposed schedule and mind-set, which he endured for three decades in the advertising world. Much of Fella's current design efforts continue his attempt to *"take the conceit out of typefaces."* He does this using every device he can imagine, from reversals and hugely exaggerated, irregular spacing to ragged margins and mixed-up fonts. He even produced a piece using only those fonts whose names rhymed *"to explore the resulting aesthetics,"* he explains. Though Fella himself never took up the computer as a design tool, his photostat work later inspired a generation of digital font designers to create battered and crude typefaces on their sophisticated machines. As LEWIS BLACKWELL wrote, Fella has *"developed a range of techniques that contradict the notion of 'slick design.' . . . As an antidote, he presents an aesthetic which is anti-aesthetic"* (*20th Century Type,* Rizzoli, 1992).

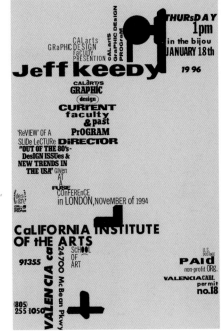

CalArts Presents, *1994–96.*

The move away from professional practice helped liberate Fella's progressive typographic and design output. The announcements he created for CalArts' guest lecturers represent an intermingling of the visiting artist's style with Fella's own quirkiness.

which is anti-aesthetic" (*20th Century Type*, Rizzoli, 1992).

Teaching at CalArts has allowed Fella to directly influence many of tomorrow's potential design stars. He challenges them by preaching the notions of order, balance, and continuity in his classes, then telling his students to take these rules and *"disturb, distract, and distort"* everything about them. *"When you're a student, you want to deal with possibilities,"* he urges them. *"Later on, you will have to deal with necessities."*

Fella has undoubtedly affected how designers will design for years to come, but he is not through creating yet. Still, he is modest about his accomplishments. He puts his impact on the profession's history in perspective by comparing his achievements so far with those of European maverick WOLFGANG WEINGART, who pioneered New Wave Typography in the late 1960s. Through his work and his teachings at the Basel School of Design, Weingart has influenced many designers, including APRIL GREIMAN and DANIEL FRIEDMAN, with his continuous challenging of the Swiss school's dogmatic rules and orderliness. *"Weingart's work was an explosion in the Linotype factory,"* Fella remarks. *"He's a late modernist, while my work is postmodernist. It's the difference between connotation and denotation. Weingart's work is wonderful, but it's done. The statement has been made, it's an endpoint."* (In fact, Weingart politely rejected an invitation to be included in this book, saying, *"I have not worked for over ten years anymore in the 'Radical,' either for clients, myself, or as an instructor. We will probably not find too many Radical designers in this world."*)

Fella believes, however, that although history moves on, people remain current as long as they are inquisitive and continue experimenting. That's why he adds, unlike Weingart's work, *"My work is a beginning point; it's still going on."*

tibor kalman

M&Co. Labs, Inc., New York, New York

the content provider

TIBOR KALMAN appeared on a major network's nightly news show in 1997 to give his expert opinion on whether current cigarette advertising was encouraging youthful smokers. He felt strongly that it did, and at the end of the segment he boldly offered to create, for free, a new cigarette package devoid of brand identity. To date, the tobacco industry has not taken him up on his proposal.

Other designers may be reluctant to alienate an industry whose well-heeled clients could easily keep their studios running for years. Yet Kalman is fearless when it comes to voicing his controversial views, ready to tackle nearly anyone over any issue. In Kalman's mind, money is what separates the innovators from the followers, and he points an accusing finger at corporations and clients who use funding to control design. *"Designers are very often afraid to challenge their clients, to rethink things, and, most importantly, to quit jobs because of creative restraints,"* he remarks. *"If you believe in your ideas, money will follow. If you pursue money, you should fail."* Kalman applies this sort of thinking to his own work. He takes on only projects for clients he deems progressive enough to allow the artistic freedom that permits him to produce conscientious work.

Kalman's design attitude has been shaped by an assortment of talents, from the Russian Constructivists to CHARLES and RAY EAMES and ANDY WARHOL. He borrows Warhol's sense of wit and humor, the Eames's elegance, and the Constructivists' brightly colored geometric shapes and expressive typography, and he incorporates them into his own productions. However, politics is undoubtedly Kalman's biggest catalyst. In one of his most noted projects, a 1988 music video for DAVID BYRNE and the Talking Heads' song "(Nothing But) Flowers," text wraps around the musicians' faces spelling out politically conscious admonitions, including "Number of 14 year olds currently detained in South Africa: 290." As creative director, he turned *Colors*, the magazine Benetton uses to promote its clothing, into a forum for controversial issues such as racism. Even his own firm's Christmas promotions are

Restaurant Florent menu board, *1986.*

This menu board for Restaurant Florent is an early example of Kalman's explorations into degenerative typography. The design is a perfect complement to the restaurant's own charm and character. A newspaper ad campaign also adopted this attitude of simplicity.

APRIL FLORENT
ANYTHING CAN HAPPEN

TEMPS 46-52
RECORD HI 90 LO 12
11 DAYS O' RAIN

GREEN MARKETS IT'S SPRING!
UNION SQUARE
WED FRI SAT

B'WAY N WORTH
FRI S

GO EARLY

LAMB W. NEW POTA OES
SCRAMBLED EGGS

FLORENT

outlets for Kalman's political views. In 1989, he sent those on his mailing list twenty-six
dollars in cash and envelopes preaddressed to the Gay Men's Health Crisis, the Coalition for
the Homeless—and the Fund to Reduce the Federal Deficit.

Kalman's political inclination is a result of his upbringing. He was born in Hungary, the son
of a "privileged" mechanical engineer, and his family was forced to flee the country during the 1956 Communist
takeover. The Kalmans eventually landed in Poughkeepsie, New York, where the newness of living in a foreign
land embedded in the eight-year-old boy a keen curiosity that prompted him
to question everything, which he still does today. Indeed, his first step in the
design process is to decide whether the project's actual frame of reference
needs altering—that is, has the client determined the project's true problem?

New Republic ad, *1987.*

Design traditionalists, especially those who take issue with
Kalman's provocative demeanor, are always quick to point out that, in reality,
he is not a true designer—he's an art director. He merely tells others how to
design, rather than design himself. Kalman is even faster to correct them, saying that he is neither. He is, instead, a "content provider" who deals not only
with form but with a project's content and context. M&Co.'s 42nd Street project, for instance, involved no actual design. Instead, New York asked Kalman
to imagine how the famed street should appear after its revitalization, then to
develop guidelines for *others* to use during the process. The street was once a
tourist mecca, drawing people by the thousands to its elegant theaters and movie
houses, but by the 1990s it had degenerated into a seedy area populated by peep
shows, porn shops, and criminals. Kalman's goal was to save what most considered the good part of 42nd Street—its eccentric personality—and ensure
that it did not end up as just another ubiquitous, chain store–lined thorough-
fare. *"Forty-second Street was about making the street a democratic place where all
New Yorkers go,"* Kalman says of his mission. In the end, even the most vocal
opponents of the revitalization agreed that M&Co.'s plan was a success.

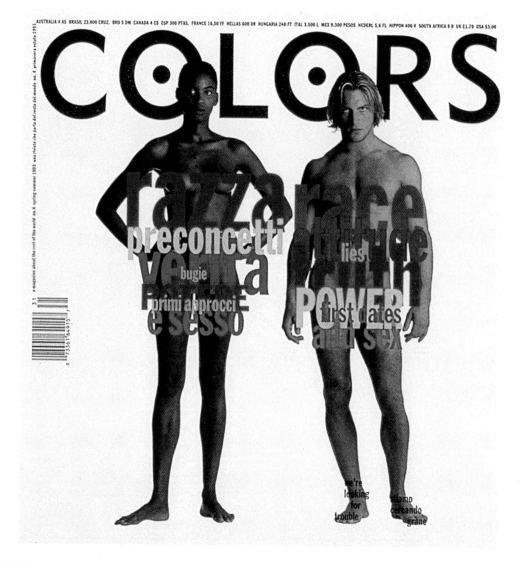

Colors No. 9, *1993.*

As creative director, Kalman refused to limit Colors, *a Benetton promotional magazine, to the pedestrian topics and self-serving articles most often found in such publications. The issue shown here deals with racism. One of the articles compares body parts of various races and portrays a "composited" person developed on computer using parts of people from different races and nationalities.*

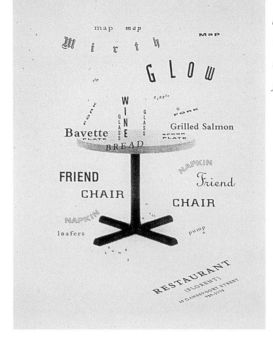

Postcards, *1990.*

These cards for Restaurant Florent offer a prime

example of Kalman's wit and sense of irony and his affinity

for vernacular visual elements.

In a way, Kalman provided 42nd Street with the proper window dressing—a role for which he is eminently qualified. After graduating college in the late 1960s with a degree in journalism, Kalman found a job working part-time for a chain of bookstores that eventually became Barnes and Noble. His duty was to sit in the basement and arrange books in alphabetical order. To escape boredom, he volunteered for a number of other tasks, including taking charge of the display windows and creating in-store signage. *"They really had no one else to do it, so they let me,"* he recalls. When the company expanded, Kalman turned his *"dorky, pseudo kind of job"* into a full-time position. A couple of years later, the bookstore hired him some assistants—"real designers" who were better at execution than he was. What they couldn't do, however, was match Kalman's quirky conceptual inventions. So he provided the ideas and direction, while the designers used their skills to pull them off.

That ability—to take apart each design challenge and then reassemble it in a surprising new way—is Kalman's forte. First and foremost, there must be a memorable (often humorous or witty) idea developed for each project, then M&Co.'s designers can concentrate on the visual translation. *"I think that the role of a designer is to be a communicator,"* Kalman commented in *Creativity* magazine (January 13, 1992), *"and part of the problem is that designers tend not to make a contribution to content."* Designers should *"ignore all the things that make design boring,"* he adds, *"and stretch for what makes it valuable—its cultural impact. Every time a designer doesn't take advantage of that, it's a waste of paper and opportunity. And that's a tragedy."*

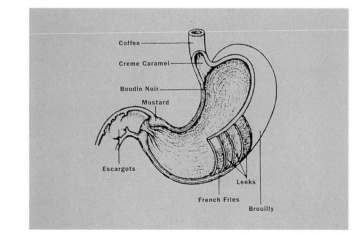

katherine mccoy

McCoy & McCoy, Buena Vista, Colorado

geological layers

KATHERINE MCCOY is not bent on upsetting design's traditional apple cart. She doesn't even consider her work radical, although she knows there are designers who feel she is ruining the profession by disregarding its cherished truisms of orderliness and readability. On the other hand, McCoy is certain some students during her twenty-five years as cochair of the esteemed design program at Cranbrook Academy of Art (Bloomfield Hills, Michigan) found her work conservative. *"If a commitment to change is radical, I guess one could describe my design as radical,"* she says. *"Each project should be a step forward into uncharted territory, an exploration of new potentials for design solutions."*

McCoy's work is characterized by a sense of order and structure in form and typography, a reduction of elements offset by complexity, and a love of black and white. Her design process is like a geological layering of past experiences. Typically, she begins with her earliest influences—the analysis and clearly delivered message structuring of the Swiss school. She then moves forward. *"Like the earth's crust, those layers aren't always neat and horizontal,"* she said, with her work's forms and processes interacting *"like the mesas and canyons in Utah,"* which she loves to explore in her leisure time. A 1986 poster McCoy created to announce the appointment of GRAHAM MARKS as Cranbrook's new head of the ceramics department is an appropriate example of how her processes merge. Crisp, legible text spelling out the department's philosophical approach is presented in strict, orderly columns across the top quarter of the 28-by-22-inch sheet, demonstrating a classic Swiss methodology. Yet, there is a hint of a break from the strict Swiss structure with McCoy's overlapping of "Cranbrook" and "Ceramics" in the poster's headline and with a switching of fonts in the two words. The full break from Swiss grid is witnessed in the remaining three-quarters of the poster page, which is a collagelike series of layered, interlocking, and randomly positioned images that refer to influences and themes recurring in Marks's work.

McCoy came into contact with the Swiss design approach when, fresh out of Michigan State University, she began her first job in 1967 as a junior designer with Unimark International in Detroit. Unimark was dedicated to interdisciplinary design and to bringing the European design aesthetic to the United States. As such, the studio employed a number of Swiss graphic designers who soon took McCoy under their wing. At Michigan State, where McCoy earned a degree in industrial design, the major

The Classical Language of Architecture, 1969.
McCoy's early work shows the heavy influence and Swiss school
attitude of her design mentors at Unimark International.

Graphic Artists Guild Call-for-Entries, 1972.

emphasis was on pragmatism, not style or ideology. At Unimark, however, McCoy encountered the bibles of Swiss graphic design—KARL GERSTNER'S *Designing Programmes,* ARMIN HOFMANN'S *Graphic Design Manual,* and JOSEF MÜLLER-BROCKMANN'S *Graphic Artist and His Design Problems.* At the time, they represented a new way of thinking, where style and ideology were vital factors in a project's visual makeup. McCoy's fellow designers stressed minimalism, urging her to keep her work "clean" and to consider design a science. They even wore white lab coats at work. Designer MASSIMO VIGNELLI— noted for, among other things, developing furniture manufacturer Knoll International's corporate identity and for his signage for the New York subway system—headed Unimark's New York office and periodically critiqued their work. McCoy credits this time for helping her gather a strong portfolio and *"a head full of ideas that grounded me as a graphic designer."*

By the time McCoy became cochair of Cranbrook's design program in 1971 (along with her husband, Michael, an industrial designer), she had pursued Swiss refinement in her work "as far as was fruitful," she says. She now began to focus on loosened grids, developing a new complexity of form and interplay among the text, images, and structure. Beyond the Swiss school, design's historic influences had previously not factored much into McCoy's work, but now they became an important component. *"The discovery of design history, stimulated by teaching, began to take my work away from simple Swiss to something much more complex. I think it was pretty much a structural exploration. It was about colliding grids, overlapping structures, what people like to call 'layering' now,"* McCoy told design writer KARRIE JACOBS (*AIGA Journal,* issue 2, 1994). She moved on from Unimark's minimalist doctrine to probe the complexities of early twentieth-century revolutionaries like EL LISSITZKY and JAN TSCHICHOLD. She was also profoundly affected by the early 1970s design activism of WOLFGANG

Cranbrook Academy of Art, *1975.*

In the mid-1970s, McCoy began to move away from the Swiss school of thought. She still employed clean white spaces, tight rules, and orderly blocks of pure type, but she also was beginning to experiment with overlapped imagery and opposing structures. McCoy found that "shattering the constraints of minimalism was exhilarating."

Cranbrook Academy of Art

Cranbrook academic catalog, 1979.

WEINGART, who had first taught Europe all about New Wave Typography (in which paragraphs were no longer necessarily defined by indentation, and text weight and letterspacing were adjusted at whim) and who was then altering photographic images with a printer's camera and stacking them in complex, layered collages. The confluence of all these ideas prompted *"a very stimulating interaction"* between McCoy's work and that of her students. ED FELLA, a guest critic who later became McCoy's student, and his work with American vernacular design were also major catalysts for her visual experiments, as were collaborations with architect and fellow Cranbrook instructor DANIEL LIBESKIND.

By the early 1980s, McCoy sensed that she had explored all her post-Swiss possibilities and began searching for a new laboratory, turning to French Deconstructionist writings and literary criticism for stimulation. The French theorists expanded the understanding of language to include nonverbal expression, which prompted McCoy to experiment with notions such as the audience's role in meaning's construction and the interaction of visual and verbal language forms. Their influence gelled in both the content and design of McCoy's landmark book *Cranbrook Design: The New Discourse,* published by Rizzoli in 1990, in which she explored the visual and verbal structures of communication. These concepts continue to affect her work today, leading her to conclude that designers must reach beyond impartial presentation and inject their work with symbolic meaning. In effect, she believes, designers are the interpreters and communicators of cultural values.

In 1996, after twenty-three years, the McCoys left Cranbrook for part-time teaching positions at the Institute of Design at the Illinois Institute of Technology (formerly the New Bauhaus) in Chicago. They spend the rest of their days at their studio in Colorado. Teaching allows McCoy to formalize assumptions from earlier visual tests; her professional practice lets her try them out for clients, including Cranbrook, the World Expo 2000 in Hannover, Germany, and the American Center for Design's Living

Architecture Symbol and Interpretation, *1980.*

By the end of the 1970s, McCoy's work was heavily influenced by both her students and other designers, including architect and fellow Cranbrook instructor Daniel Libeskind. The playful geometric shapes, textures, and colors of the Memphis style of postmodern design are evident in this poster McCoy created in collaboration with Libeskind.

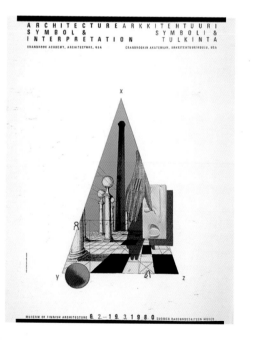

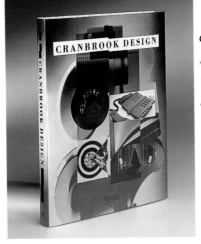

Cranbrook Design: The New Discourse, 1990.

McCoy had advanced to fully uninhibited, complex explorations by the start of the 1990s. This book represents a milestone in her own work and that of other Radical designers, with both its content and visual style probing new methods of communication.

Surfaces Conference (for which she designed the 1998 logotype and one of the marketing pieces, as well as provided design direction for other conference materials). *"But even as I apply these theories, I hope that my current work retains layers of evidence from all its earlier stages,"* she remarks. *"A designer's work should be an integrated whole, not a schizophrenic pendulum swinging from one influence to another."*

MASSIMO VIGNELLI once warned a graduate student that *"Cranbrook was the most dangerous design school in the world."* It was meant as a criticism, yet McCoy took it as a compliment of the highest sort. *"I think we should all be 'dangerous' designers with a risk-taking stance, a willingness to abandon conventions to break new ground and take that next step,"* she says. Innovation, she believes, demands an intellectual and creative alertness and a vision of graphic design's potential.

Cranbrook Ceramics, 1987.

McCoy created this poster to announce the appointment of Graham Marks as the chair of Cranbrook's ceramics department by projecting slides of staged photograph montages over one of Marks's artworks. His spiral-and-coil ceramic process is reiterated by an engraving of a butterfly tongue, a coiled prehistoric Japanese pot, and a photograph of him building a coiled piece.

Choice, 1992.

Like most other designers, McCoy's work entered a digital realm in the 1990s, as seen in this piece she created for The Electronic Exquisite Corpse *brochure. By the middle of the decade, however, she and her students were returning to the "rematerialism" of the precomputer days.*

paula scher

Pentagram, New York, New York

Best of Jazz, *1979.*

The assignment was to fit twenty names on a poster, make it big, and do it fast and cheap. The result helped reestablish typography as a major design element and secured Scher's spot as a leading voice in the profession.

it's in the timing

PAULA SCHER, whose deeply conceptual work and inclination to take risks have made her one of the most influential and highly regarded designers of the late-twentieth century, believes Radicalism is contingent on being in the right place at the right time. *"It's not necessarily a matter of being the first to create something, or to be experimental,"* Scher says. *"Being 'radical' is a matter of timeliness, too. You have to be doing something at a specific point where it can be influential, where it is different from everything else going on at that time."*

A good example of the role of timing is Scher's Best of Jazz poster, created while she was art director at CBS Records during the 1970s. Using what was at the time an unorthodox approach, she focused on typography as the main visual element. In today's design climate this is nothing unusual, but during the 1970s it was a designer's job to hide the type as much as possible: illustrations and photographs dominated; typography faded into the background. If the type was obvious at all, it was always *"centered, soft, and sweet,"* Scher remarks. The jazz poster, however, featured bold, chunky blocks of type set at grid-defying angles, consuming 90 percent of the poster's space.

Initially, the Best of Jazz was rejected by every design exhibition in which it was entered. It wasn't until 1982, when it was featured in the *Just Type* show sponsored by the American Institute of Graphic Arts in New York (before the organization went national), that the design community accepted it. Soon, its influence was pervasive. Today, Best of Jazz is considered a visual landmark, and Scher is praised for her propagation of type-driven style. This, however, is something she later considered a double-edged sword. *"The poster became a stylistic noose around my neck,"* she notes.

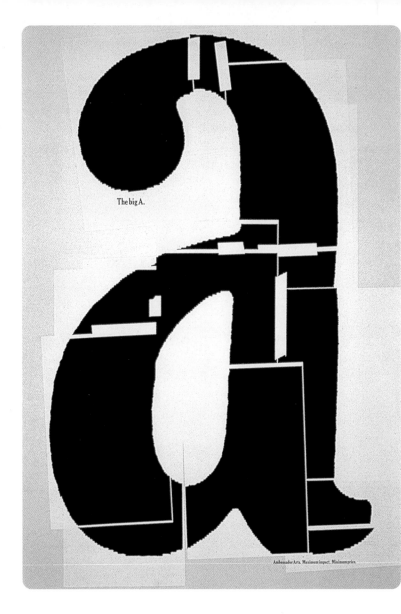

The big A.

Ambassador Arts. Maximum impact. Minimum price.

The Big A, *1991.*

To promote the silk screening capabilities of Ambassador Arts, Scher made a huge 36-by-50-inch symbol using a photocopier to repeatedly enlarge a typewritten Cheltenham character. She then layered the pages atop one another to form a collage, which she printed on oversized sheets of newsprint to demonstrate the quality of the silk screening. Subtle differences in the shades of white are evident in spite of the flimsy newsprint.

Trust Elvis, *1981.*

Scher's sense of humor comes through in this promotional poster, which plays off the mystique of Elvis Costello.

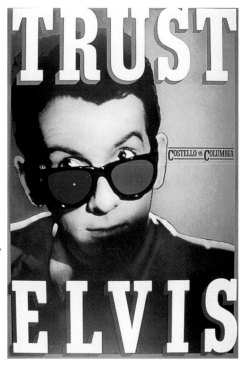

The Diva Is Dismissed, *1994.*

This poster, created for Jenifer Lewis's one-woman show
at the Public Theater, follows the theater's design guidelines
to juxtapose photography and type.

Though Scher resists being pigeonholed into any design category, her creations are connected by a distinctive visual language, fashioned from a wide body of influences. First and foremost is her husband and mentor, illustrator and designer SEYMOUR CHWAST, a founding member of Push Pin Studio. Chwast's blending of Art Nouveau, Art Deco, and Victorian forms with a potent sense of irony and humor has cast a strong shadow on Scher and her work.

Individuality is ensured by matching clients' needs to their personalities. The new identity created for the Public Theater in 1994 is a good example. The Public Theater had long flourished under the directorship of JOSEPH PAPP, but after his death in 1991 the dynamic organization lost its edge. When George C. Wolfe was appointed its new producer in 1992, he sought to reinvigorate the theater by enlarging the scope and diversity of its productions and audience, and by promoting it as streetwise, timely, and accessible. Scher took Wolfe's quest literally. Under her guidance, Pentagram developed a varied but cohesive graphic language that reflects the active, unconventional, and almost graffiti-like quality of "street" typography. The program aptly expresses the nature of the theater and establishes an identity uniquely its own.

The singular manner in which Scher approaches design comes partially from her education at the Tyler School of Art in Philadelphia, where she trained as an illustrator. After graduation, she moved to New York to illustrate, but soon realized she was a better designer. *"My illustrating and drawing were never very good, but my ideas were,"* she comments. So she accepted a job at Random House, designing children's books. She moved on to CBS Records, eventually becoming its East Coast art director at the age of twenty-six. *"On the way, I learned how to be a graphic designer,"* she says. Just as timing is a defining factor in Radicalism, it was instrumental in shaping Scher's design spirit. *"I started my career in 1970 when it was a very wide open profession,"* she says. *"You could bounce around and try things out."* The tendency to always reach for something new still guides her work today.

The Public Theater, *1994.*

Venus, 1996.

Venus is a play that tells the story of the Venus Hottentot, an African woman with huge buttocks who moved to England in 1810 to become a side-show novelty. She eventually inspired her own form of nineteenth-century design—the bustle. Scher cleverly plays off the woman's remarkable characteristic in this poster.

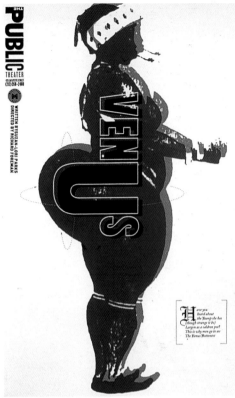

THE PUBLIC THEATER/NEW YORK SHAKESPEARE FESTIVAL PRESENTS

BRING IN 'DA **NOISE** BRING IN 'DA **FUNK**

"VISUALLY STUNNING!
AT TIMES THE DANCING SEEMS LIKE AN ASSAULT ON THE FEET. THEY DANCE ON THEIR TOES, THEIR HEELS, SEEMINGLY ON THEIR ANKLES, INVARIABLY WITH RELENTLESS ABANDON."

"THIS EPIC POEM OPENS THE DOOR THROUGH WHICH TAP CAN ENTER THE 21ST CENTURY. IT SLAMS RAW RHYTHMS INTO YOUR HEART!"

MEDITATION ON TAP,

"A JOYOUS CELEBRATION! THE CAST IS SUPERB!"

"A JOYOUS MEDITATION ON TAP,

WHAT IS 'NOISE/FUNK'? IT IS DANCE THEATER. IT IS MUSICAL THEATER. IT IS EPIC THEATER. AS DANCE. AS MUSICAL. AS THEATER AS ART, HISTORY AND ENTERTAINMENT. THERE'S NOTHING IT CANNOT AND SHOULD NOT DO.

"SAVION GLOVER IS A HUMAN DIVINING ROD OF RHYTHM. 'NOISE/FUNK' IS SO FRESH, PURE, AND ALIVE, IT VIBRATES!"

"STUNNING,"

GLOVER'S DANCING IS A REVELATION OF VIRUOSITY AND EXPRESSIVENESS. THIS MUSICAL HAS BROUGHT BACK 'DA BEAT."

HEROIC!

GEORGE C. WOLFE AND SAVION GLOVER HAVE CONCOCTED A SHORT-HAND VERSION OF AMERICAN HISTORY, IN WHICH THE BEAT OF DANCE IS EQUATED WITH SOMETHING LIKE AN UNSTOPPABLE LIFE FORCE. THE MOST ORIGINAL MUSICAL PRODUCTION OF THE SEASON."

"GEORGE WOLFE AND SAVION GLOVER ARE THE INSPIRED CREATORS OF THIS BREATH-TAKING AND REVELATORY SHOW WHICH RESTORES EMOTIONAL CONTENT TO SHOW-BIZ CHOREOGRAPHY IN WAYS CURRENTLY UNMATCHED ON BROADWAY STAGES. ITS RHYTHMS WILL PULSE IN YOUR BLOODSTREAM LONG AFTER ITS OVER!

"'NOISE' ROCKETS THE AMERICAN MUSICAL INTO THE MODERN AGE!"

CALL TELE-CHARGE IN NY NJ/CT 212-239-6200 OUTSIDE NY METRO AREA 800-432-7250

THE AMBASSADOR THEATRE 219 WEST 49TH STREET BEGINS APRIL 9TH

Bring in Da Noise, Bring in Da Funk, 1996.

The history of African American rhythm told through dancer/choreographer Savion Glover's explosive street-tap style was a hit at the Public Theater before moving to Broadway. The Broadway campaign features the same Wood typefaces used for the Public Theater's identity, interacting with Richard Avedon's photograph of a dancing Glover. The image is amplified by the starkness of the surrounding white space. Critics' comments bombard Glover's image.

rick valicenti

Thirst, Barrington, Illinois

the ardent crusader

RICK VALICENTI is possibly the most impassioned designer working today. His intense emotion and professional devotion are manifested in both his design creations and his zealous personality. Valicenti does not hesitate to infuse a client's promotion with his evocative fine art; he is not afraid to cry in front of hundreds of peers, overcome by his love for design. When Valicenti broke down in tears while addressing the 1991 American Institute of Graphic Arts (AIGA) National Design Conference, his colleagues reacted with either indifference, embarrassment, or cynicism. In an *AIGA Journal* review, a critic suggested that Valicenti's outburst was *"emotion as promotion."* Valicenti remembers those months following the conference as the worst in his career. Particularly distressing to him was that so few understood the burning passion he feels for design. Valicenti took their apathy as a sign the profession was in great trouble, and it made him more determined than ever to succeed in his crusade to reinject his work with artistic spirit.

That decision resulted in a torrential flow of design inspired by *"family, friends, television, pop culture, Elvis, and Madonna's baby"*—in short, Valicenti's environment. Mainly, though, he reached into his soul for direction and was rewarded with some of the most remarkable and controversial designs to appear in the 1990s. The main criticism of those who dislike Valicenti's work is that it is more about personal art than a client's visual marketing needs and, thus, does the client a disservice—and gives design a bad name. Foremost among the pieces that have caused such controversy is a series of promotions he created in the early 1990s for Gilbert Paper. Probably the most contentious of those is a booklet called *Give and Take* (1993), which is packed with artwork by Valicenti and guest artists that says nothing about the project. Viewers seem to either love it or hate it; no one remains neutral. BRENDA WILHELMSON and TERRY KATTLEMAN, writing in *Creativity* (issue 3, 1993), said the promotion *"may well claim the title of the farthest-out*

Enter, *1989.*

This call for entries, created for The STA 100 Show, features ten different photographers whose work appears digital, though the brochure was created without using computers.

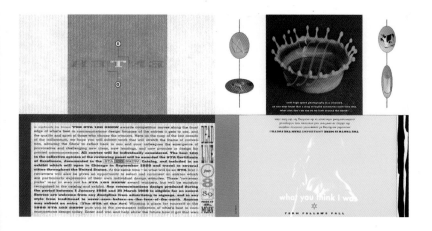

Add a Little Magic, *1992.*

This technological training center schedule demonstrates what

students can hope to learn there. Interior spreads display

colorful, futuristic, occasionally cartoonish imagery. Simple blocks of clearly

legible text counterbalance the chaotic complexity.

Give and Take, *1993.*

Valicenti calls his work "engaging and expressive," qualities clearly demonstrated in this booklet for Gilbert Paper.

The promotion proved controversial in the design community because it was filled with the personal art of Valicenti and

several "guest" artists, rather than focused on the product's attributes.

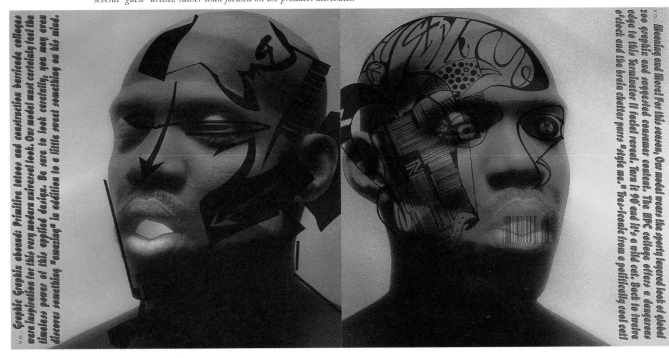

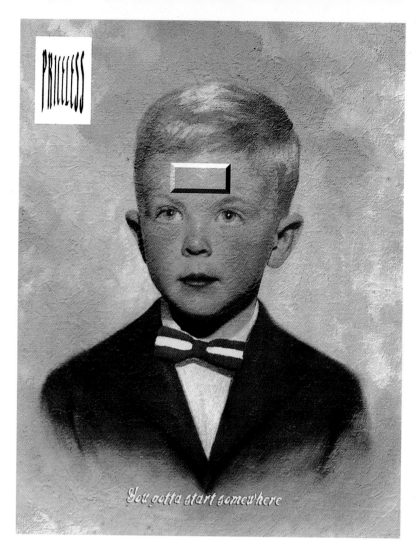

PRICELESS

You gotta start somewhere

FISHER BICYCLE
801 West Madison Street
Waterloo WI 53594, USA
toll free 1.800.472.4763 (US only)
telephone 1.414.478.3537
facsimile 1.414.478.3536
www.FisherBikes.com

You gotta end up somewhere

MARLIN

Fisher Bicycle, *1996.*

The kinetic interplay between text and photographs perfectly matches the nature of this catalog's products.
The piece also exploits the personality of Fisher Bicycle's owner Gary Fisher: the front cover bears a portrait of him
as a boy, the picture of innocence; the back carries a recent image of Fisher—sporting a beret, a goatee, and a
smirk—that's been haphazardly plastered across the same portrait from the front cover.

Thirstype, 1996.

Valicenti and designer Patricking illustrated and designed this mailer announcing two new fonts in the collection of Thirstype, Valicenti's type house. The result is what one might expect from Hieronymus Bosch if he'd had access to a computer.

paper promos around." A classroom of college juniors at a highly respected graphic design program pinned it to the wall and proceeded to critically rip it apart during a seminar on "good" design. They were appalled that the brochure was devoid of classic Swiss design standards in favor of wordplay, barely decipherable text, personal art, and enigmatic imagery. In spite of the mixed reactions, Gilbert Paper loved its promotion. Valicenti had positioned the company as savvy about design and oriented toward the needs of designers. The mill is still not certain how much paper Valicenti's work sold, but he had redefined its marketing strategy for years to come.

Because of its openmindedness, Gilbert is just the type of client Valicenti prefers. At one time in his career, the designer took on several large corporations who did not have Gilbert's trust in his ability and who demanded a more traditional marketing approach for their projects. Fed up with that sort of thinking, Valicenti reorganized his studio in 1988 and laid off all but a core crew. He also changed the name from R. Valicenti Design, which had been established seven years earlier, to Thirst and, shortly after, moved from the heart of Chicago to a small community about two hours away. Surrounded by a staff made up mostly of family and by working only for clients who share his appetite for innovation, he has further distanced himself from Corporate America and eliminated those conservative companies from his client roster. With a smaller operation to support, he can now afford to be choosy about the projects he accepts.

Valicenti has come to grips with those bleak days after the 1991 AIGA Conference and realized that a willingness to *"be naked"* in public is what sets him apart. That attitude is accompanied by an insatiable curiosity and a perverse sense of humor. Valicenti has been able to convince his clients of the importance of these qualities; they are his collaborators in the process of invention. Valicenti's mantra today is, *"Trust our instincts and jump."*

innovators

jackson boelts
eric boelts
kerry stratford

Boelts Bros. Associates, Tucson, Arizona

design by nature

If BOELTS BROS. ASSOCIATES were located in one of the so-called design centers, its members would surely travel in that small clique reserved for the profession's preeminent celebrities. After all, JACKSON BOELTS is credited by such a design luminary as DAVID CARSON as not only his mentor but as the person who first lured him into the field. There's also no doubt that if Boelts Bros. were located any place other than where it is, the work coming from its three talents would not be what it is.

Living and working in Arizona's desert has had a huge impact on how they create; it's a setting that Jackson Boelts once described as *"almost like the bottom of an ocean floor"* where unique plants and animals have prospered in the harsh environment through adaptation. The designers, too, have adapted, producing work that is a blend of technology, nature, and the artistic influences of Native American and Mexican cultures. An almost scenic beauty abounds in much that they create, with muted, earthy hues dotted by occasional splashes of brilliance, like the stunning wildflowers that appear from seemingly nowhere to pepper the pale desert sands. Primitive, almost metaphysical figures—some animal in nature, others obviously influenced by kachina dolls and other sacred Native American fetishes—float playfully about. Frequently, a sense of whimsy prevails. For example, the studio's invoices sport "begging wolves" icons; the Egyptian gods for good luck adorn its estimate forms. Yet, whether fanciful or serious, their work is always driven by a strong concept—an idea that results in a drawing requiring just minutes to execute may take weeks of gestation.

Most of all, living and working in their sequestered Southwestern habitat makes it easy for the partners to be individuals, unimpeded by the rules and pressure of the New York or Los Angeles design arenas. It all comes down, they say, to a matter of choice. *"You get to chart your own course here, as opposed to following what everybody else seems to be doing,"* ERIC BOELTS remarks.

That's not to say the three are unaware of what is happening outside Arizona's arid borders. They cite widespread influences on their work. Architecture and fashion are the inspirations for partner KERRY STRATFORD. The Boelts mention the European poster artists, GRAPUS, TAKENOBU IGARASHI, MILTON GLASER, and their former design school teachers as

Vision, 1992.

This poster portrays the designers' feelings about the Los Angeles rioting sparked by the acquittal of the police in the Rodney King beating incident. It was created using a combination of high-tech and traditional techniques—the figure was drawn with a felt-tip pen while type was fashioned on computer in Aldus FreeHand—then it was printed on a two-color press to create the split-fountain gradation.

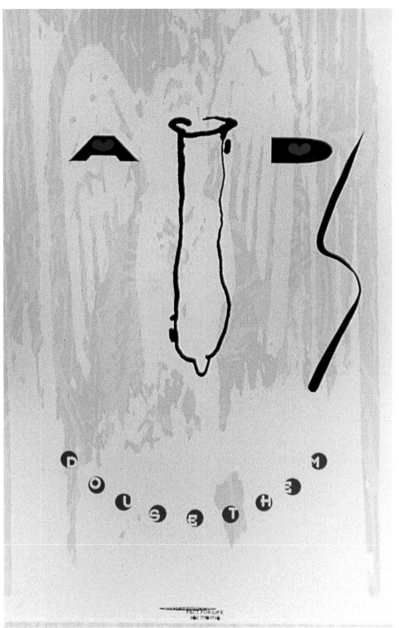

AIDS poster, 1994.

This very personal project was inspired by the death of a friend from AIDS. The original "face" was designed on a napkin, then the poster built around it. Photographs and drawings of angels appear in the background, including one done in a tinted screen and another in a tinted varnish.

Polo, 1994.

Boelts Bros. has created a pro bono poster for this Tucson annual fundraiser for years; they receive much satisfaction from giving something back to the community.

Orts, 1990.

To show appreciation for this avant-garde Tucson dance troupe, Boelts Bros. created its entire identity system as well as a series of oversized posters. The poster here was created by drawing and scratching on original slides, then scanning them directly to negatives. The two photographs were dropped into a mask, as the negative material did not cover the entire poster area. Typography was created in Aldus FreeHand.

Ringo Starr, 1992.

This poster for a charity concert needed to showcase the headliner in the best light, which was not easy since the photographs sent to the studio from London revealed Starr's poor dental work. The designers fixed his teeth by scanning the photograph in low-resolution at a reduced size, then enlarging it. The image was then combined in Aldus FreeHand with hand-drawn visuals using a Wacom™ tablet. The resulting cartoonlike feel lends itself to the irreverent Starr and his music.

having a profound impact on their work. They also prefer the European approach to design, which considers all design disciplines as part of one entity, rather than the separatist mentality in the United States that pits fine arts against graphic design and architecture. Such thinking comes through in the announcement they created for the 1996 USA/Poland Poster Exhibition call-for-entries. Though composited on the computer, the poster plays off the handmade genre of European posters by using Jackson's whimsical, hand-drawn images as its basis.

Tucson's relaxed pace also affects their work because it allows them time to be introspective, contemplating how their careers and lifestyles meld, and where they want to be in coming years. They consider themselves Radicals, but not in any ordinary sense of the word. Instead, their revolutionary thinking is manifested in how their design work merges with their lifestyle. Each studio member is encouraged to devote time to personal causes (AIDS and the arts are high on their list), and as such, pro bono projects make up a bulk of their work. They also are selective about their paying clients, opting for those whose projects merge with their own artistic inclinations rather than those that offer merely a lot of money.

In the end, the Boelts Bros. designers believe, innovation is all a matter of perspective. You can either look at design as a job or craft, or you can look at it as a very intimate, emotional, liberating form of communication—one that allows you to *"venture out on the ledge,"* Jackson Boelts says, *"and stretch for the apple."* Most of all, their rebel attitude allows them to be comfortable in the knowledge that they are not designers driven by art, but artists who just happen to design.

End of Summer, *1993.*

A strong concept and technique were needed for David Carson's eclectic designs. The idea for this Jackson Boelts illustration centered around crossing out the sun; the technique involved using pastels over an airbrushed watercolor base.

margo chase

Margo Chase Design, Los Angeles, California

the progressive gothic

MARGO CHASE reaches centuries into the past for help in formulating her progressive visual vocabulary. She is continually reinterpreting medieval manuscripts, Gothic architecture, calligraphy, and alchemical imagery, and then intermingling the results with more contemporary stimuli, such as MAN RAY's photography and PIET ZWART's typography. The result is a diverse body of award-winning design whose appearance occasionally borders on the macabre. Yet even in its most extreme form, her work exhibits elegance and finesse.

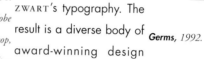

Perpetual Flux and Change, 1990.

The lettering looks hand-drawn, but it was actually built in Adobe Illustrator. The entire composition was assembled in Adobe Photoshop, where the swirling type was created using the twirl filter.

Germs, *1992.*

Part of her work's unusual appearance is an outgrowth of Chase's intense interest in science and medicine, her original career choice. She earned a bachelor's degree in biology from California Polytechnic Institute, San Luis Obispo, then moved on to the University of California, San Francisco, where she took graduate courses in medical illustration. Eventually, Chase found medical illustration *"too limiting"* and turned to graphic design. After several years of freelancing, she opened her own studio in 1986, where her iconoclastic type treatments—distinguished by a hybrid mixture of existing fonts, customized digital fonts, and lettering painstakingly fashioned by hand—soon set her work apart. The poster Germs (the title comes from Chase's term for her inspirations), created in 1992 to announce her lecture at Alberta College of Art, Calgary, is a good example of how her influences and processes merge. In it, Chase used the digital typeface Bradley, which she originally fabricated for a client's stationery system. Bradley was inspired by a font created in 1927 by Czech designer VOJTĚCH

Band of Angels CD, *1992.*

The wing icon and lettering for this CD package were hand-sketched, then built in Adobe Illustrator using the sketch as a template.

Lettering was imported into Adobe Photoshop and masked so that the photo image could be darkened and ghosted within the text.

The background cherub photograph was scanned, manipulated, and colorized in Adobe Photoshop.

Vitriol–The Acid Test, 1994.

Historically, vitriol refers to an alchemist's formula for the process of transmutation (the attempt to transform base metals into gold). Today, the word denotes something with a caustic quality, and Chase believes it is very suited to the design process, so she used it in this piece she created for Letter Arts Review. *"As designers and artists, exposing our work to public comment is the acid test by which we are judged," she comments. "For the less secure, criticism may stop us from creating at all; for the more experienced, it can be a positive process by which we grow. Criticism that may at first feel caustic can help us to discover 'gold,' by leading us to refine and analyze our work."*

PREISSIG that Chase found in a 1920s book of Czechoslovakian type creations done by designers for local type foundries; she often uses the book to inspire her own typefaces. Chase's interpretation of Preissig's font is made up entirely of straight lines, none of which are true verticals or horizontals. This construction gives the font its unusual appearance and a practical versatility, too, by allowing it to be easily manipulated without appearing distorted. The background illustration in the poster is a combination of a gargoyle photograph and an old painting of the Madonna, reflecting Chase's affinity for medieval elements. The moiré pattern that appears behind the images in the right half of the poster is the product of a more contemporary "stimulus"—a mistake that occurred during the printing process. Chase had sent a half-size digital file to the printer, but never got a chance to proof the final output. Though the moiré was unintentional, she liked the result.

Many of Chase's customers today are in the music and entertainment industries—she's created logos for musicians Madonna, Bonnie Raitt, Prince, Mariah Carey, and Santana, and posters for movies including *Goldeneye, Dragonheart,* and Bram Stoker's *Dracula.* Signage for hotels and entertainment complexes, food packaging, editorial work, and promotional materials for snowboard manufacturers and fashion houses are just some of the other industries on her design roster. All come to Chase seeking a precocious dose of innovation.

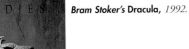
Bram Stoker's Dracula, *1992.*

IDEA *magazine, 1994.*

Chase's ability to create digital fonts with a
hand-drawn appearance is demonstrated in the custom
lettering she created for this magazine cover.
The lettering was inspired by Islamic calligraphy.

Marvin Gaye, The Master CD, *1995.*

This special four-CD anthology featured a bound-in, sixty-eight-page booklet. Chase's studio created a custom digital font for the project called Fatboy (used along with Triplex and Matrix Script), which was inspired by 1970s-style bold and ugly type.

Chase begins each project employing *"traditional"* design sensibilities, then stretches for a way to surpass them. She seeks to eliminate the routine and pedestrian without breaking down what's functional or valuable. Market research plays a huge role in this process, with the studio assembling all of the information it can on a subject. For an album project for Loreena McKennitt, for instance, Chase read about Marco Polo and a book on the history of books that McKennitt recommended; to get ideas for the movie project *The Crow,* she studied modern Chinese politics and visited San Francisco's Chinatown district to view firsthand that culture's advertising and graphic design ephemera.

Critics say Chase's designs and typefaces are *"too pointy"*; others, simply, *"scary."* Granted, her Gothic persuasions occasionally result in jagged-edged, heavily stroked, almost grotesque typefaces or in peculiar icons that disclose a demonic quality (appropriately seen in a Dennis Rodman "Do or Die" graphic). But that doesn't bother Chase. *"New ideas can seem ugly at first,"* she responds. *"That's usually an indication that they really are new."*

Christmas card, 1995.

The font Envision along with two PMS and process colors

on eighty-pound white Kashmir cover stock were used for this

holiday greeting.

Craps table, 1994.

Chase's visual eccentricity resulted in a stunning identity

for the Hard Rock Hotel & Casino. Shown is a gaming table

that was part of the project.

ian anderson, mike place
nick bax, matt pyke
dave bailey, liz close, julia parfitt

The Designers Republic, Sheffield, England

nothing in common

When it comes to the disposition of THE DESIGNERS REPUBLIC, the name says it all. *"It is a declaration of independence from what we perceive to be the existing design community,"* says IAN ANDERSON, who officially founded the company in July 1986. Though at the onset the name was more of a tongue-in-cheek notice of physical separation from London's *"snobbish"* design circle than a design posture—the firm was located in the thriving music center of Sheffield, more than a hundred miles away from the London city limits—it soon came to perfectly represent the group's outlook, too. Over the years, its attitude of having *"nothing in common"* with the design establishment has gained The Designers Republic a bona fide fan club of more than six thousand devotees, an impressive client list that includes some of the world's top corporations, and the honor of being declared *"one of the most recognizable and best-loved design houses in the UK"* (*Computer Arts,* May/June 1997).

The studio's work is marked by what design commentator JEFFERY KEEDY has called a refreshing dose of *"infantilism"* for its childlike images, bold colors, and disregard for traditional design hierarchies. It also exhibits aspects of what friend and designer MALCOLM GARRETT, in an interview with RUDY VANDERLANS (*Emigre* 29, 1993), called "Hyper-Modernism" (which Anderson did not like) and "American Expressionism" (which he did like) for how they often use the strictly functional design elements more aligned with corporate identity work as building blocks for their own jokes, games, and puns. For example, about half of the projects they take on are for clients in the music and entertainment industries, including many bands made up of *"down-to-earth blokes from Next-to-Nowhere, England,"* Anderson told VanderLans. *"It appeals to our sense of humor to present such a group in big-league terms by giving their visuals the attributes of something multinational and reliable that the consumer really should know about already. This is the Emperor's New Clothes theory!"* Such thinking was the impetus behind their first record cover for Age of Chance, a band from the small town of Leeds, England. The Designers Republic team (their work is always credited collectively) developed a logo and then used it like a national emblem, pairing it with

The Orb, A Huge Ever Growing Pulsating Brain that Rules from the Center of the Ultraworld, *1989.*

This LP sleeve represents "the beginning of the end of the millennium chillout," Anderson notes, adding, "Elsewhere on the packaging NASA meets Leonardo da Vinci . . . Klaatu Berada Nikto!" Officially the first Ambient House record, the sleeve has the added distinction of being among the last of The Designers Republic's predigital designs.

Pop Will Eat Itself, This Is The Day . . . This Is The Hour . . . This Is This!, *1989.*

The studio's habit of recycling cultural icons is easily established in this record sleeve, which parodies numerous familiar logos and corporate icons to generate layers of new messages. Anderson calls the piece a mixture of "medieval information technology—digital (Mac and Amiga) vs. mechanical (paste-up and graph paper)." It also was the first time PWEI's popular Robo-head logo appeared.

Pop Will Eat Itself, 16 Different Flavours of Hell, *1993.*

Work, Buy, Consume, Die, 1995.

This 2-by-1-meter banner was commissioned for the Customized Terror Exhibition held in New York (curated by Ronald Jones of Yale University) in 1995. Anderson explains the Pepsi pun as "Generation Next versus Generation X, consumer Fascism versus the Empire of the Sun, Pop Designers Republic Cola culture. Buy nothing, pay now!" Pho-Ku Corporation is the studio's Japanese division.

multinational imagery (a globe and so on) and text (Leeds, Berlin, Detroit, New York) to suggest the band's home base and musical influences, offer a statement of intent, and provide it with an international outlook.

Yet another defining factor in the designers' work is how they will "borrow" a well-known corporate logo or icon and seamlessly incorporate it into their own work. In effect, they are recycling cultural symbols since the borrowed element is typically used in a new, often satirical and humorous context, and therefore makes its own valid artistic statement—which is very different from copying a design style or idea. Anyway, Anderson argues, there is a point at which such icons should become a part of the public domain. After all, isn't that what the corporations are striving for?

One of the best examples of its success to this end is seen in the work The Designers Republic does for the group Pop Will Eat Itself (PWEI), using the famous Pepsi symbol so well and so often that it is almost as if the band were endorsing the soft drink, and Pepsi is now traditionally served at its concerts. (Eventually, Pepsi asked the studio to stop using its logo after a group of what Anderson called *"born again Christians"* took offense at the language in PWEI's songs and threatened to boycott Pepsi if it kept up its *"sponsorship"* of the band. *"If continued use of the logo was going to get everybody concerned into hot water, then the joke wasn't funny anymore,"* he explained in the *Emigre* article.)

There are several reasons why Anderson feels a vast schism exists between him and others in the design profession. First, though as a child in London he would spend hours creating new flags for countries or new football strips, he chose to study philosophy rather than art when he entered Sheffield University in 1979. Many of his classmates were musicians who had their own bands, and Anderson followed suit until one day he realized his talents lay in managing musicians, rather than performing himself. That is when his design career informally began, creating flyers, record sleeves, and the other graphic paraphernalia that his bands needed yet could not afford to hire out. Eventually, other bands became aware of his work and asked him to design for them, too. The projects kept coming and Anderson decided to officially form a design studio. His first was called ISA-Vision (taking its name from his initials), but as the work kept coming in, Anderson decided to take on a partner (NICK PHILLIPS, who has since left the

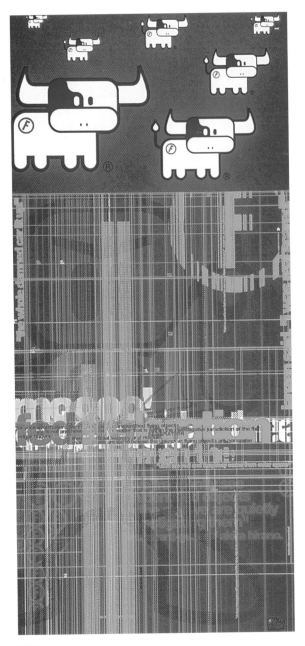

Moo, *1996.*

"UFO cows" and "bar code–based grids that reach critical mass" is Anderson's assessment of this banner created for the 1996 Sonar Exhibition at the Museum of Contemporary Art in Barcelona. The banner is based on a corporate identity that The Designers Republic developed a year earlier for Federation, a London-based television commercial production company.

Dual Layer Metal Coating, 1998.

This still is taken from animation templates for a trade video commercial that The Designers Republic created in collaboration with CWC Tokyo. The video announces a new Sony Japan digital storage system.

company) and The Designers Republic was born. *"I never actually went out to get work; people just kept coming up to me and saying they'd seen such and such, and could I do this for them?"* Anderson recalls. *"That's how it kept going for the first eighteen months, because up to that period it certainly wasn't written in stone that this was what we wanted to do forever. Designing was just what we were doing because people kept giving us work and it was a way to earn money."* Anderson believes his lack of a formal design education is partially responsible for The Designers Republic's unorthodox work. *"If you haven't been molded in the education system then you are coming to design completely on your own,"* he says, and as such are naturally imbued with a genuine naïveté that promotes a fresh approach.

Second, because he is located in Sheffield rather than in London, where most of Britain's design players reside, Anderson feels not just a physical separation from them but a cerebral one, too. Finally, because he was used to creating images for the bands he managed and because of his education, from the beginning Anderson has concentrated on creating philosophies for his clients instead of merely fashioning visual products for them. *"There always has to be something several layers beneath the surface,"* he explains, *"even if it's something that only satisfies and interests us. That's how we like to work."*

Others may strive to define The Designers Republic's style, but the studio itself—though Anderson admits they are aware of their impact on contemporary design—assumes a more nonchalant stance regarding its work. *"People want us to describe what we do, but it's just design to us,"* Anderson says. *"We don't wake up in the morning and think about how we can't wait to get to the studio and come up with some of that cutting-edge design."* There are definitely certain attitudes and approaches to The Designers Republic's work, most of which is driven by their experiences and their environment. *"There's a certain kind of filter that is made up of all those views—I think we're all aware of that,"* Anderson allows. *"But none of us is really interested or brave enough to analyze what that is, since once you do start analyzing your work, you lose the magic and the adventure."*

michael jager
giovanna di paola
david kemp

Jager Di Paola Kemp Design, Burlington, Vermont

connect

Drama, energy, and conviction characterize the creations of JAGER DI PAOLA KEMP DESIGN (JDK). The studio's work—spanning international identity systems, advertising, sales literature, collateral products, and branding (an area not typically associated with the Radical movement)—is an ongoing experiment in marrying traditional processes with emerging tools, media, and design disciplines. Yet the group manages to deliver a distinct, smart, and definite point of view for its clients, many of whom operate in youth-oriented markets such as snowboarding and active wear. Recognizing the client's brand character and acting to dramatize its traits and differences has led to the look of the studio's current work, one that is defined by an on-the-edge boldness stamped with biting humor, dynamic composition, vibrant colors, highly active photography, and swirling, kinetic lines of type.

Who the F—k is Terje?, 1996.

Like PAULA SCHER, the JDK designers believe that much innovation is a product of being in the right place at the right time. Such has been the case in the 1990s. *"We are in the midst of profound changes in consumer attitudes. Technology is driving society at a pace unparalleled in history, creating new ways of thinking, interrelationships, and global awareness,"* JDK partner MICHAEL JAGER and two of the studio's designers, DAVID COVELL and MARK SYLVESTER, told a group of students in a keynote address for the 1997 Chicago Design Student Conference. *"Today's consumers are skeptical, questioning, connected with the world, thirsting for information and change. This new consumer is keenly aware of contrived images and not easily influenced."* Not recognizing this fact, many companies have failed to reach and persuade their potential customers. JDK's designers feel that this creates a huge opportunity for those willing to explore design's impact and the changes that are occurring in product and brand characterization. Their clients are all among this group, permitting them to help fashion a point of view for the clients' products rather than merely creating attractive backdrops for them.

I like my board. Sometimes I stare at it in the mirror when I'm undressing and wonder what it would look like without any stickers like when I was a baby. Sometimes I sit at the edge of the bed and spread my legs. And stare into the mirror and wonder what others see. Sometimes I stick my feet in my bindings and wiggle it around the dark wetness and feel what a couch or a chair must feel when I'm sitting on it. I pull my feet out and I always taste it and smell it. It's hard to describe it smells like a tomato to me fresh and full of life. I love my board it is the complete summation of my life. It's the place where all the most painful things have happened. But it has given me indescribable pleasure. My ___ is the temple of learning.

BURTON

virgin catalog... 1-802-862-9900

Burton Snowboard ad, *1996.*

This advertisement keeps one reading to the end with its clever replacement of key words from Madonna's Sex book, an ode to her apparently favorite body part. The ad demonstrates JDK's focus on concept as the driving force behind the studio's work, even when it means forgoing the visual.

Power Voice logo, *1997.*

The objective was to communicate Power Voice's leadership in the integration of telecommunications and data networking. The studio accomplished this through sophisticated forms, typography, and color. Modern megaphones serve as metaphors for Power Voice's two communication paths.

Converse fall catalog, *1995.*

TDK mailer, 1995.

This attitude and awareness undoubtedly frees the designers to explore new ways of communicating, but it adds a burden: they must know their clients' audiences and products as intimately as the clients do. The studio uses interdisciplinary teams of designers, production managers, and account managers to work closely and consistently with each particular client (with an occasional swapping of team talents to meet a project's unique needs).

While all good designers, whether Radically or classically inclined, work hard to connect with their audiences, the designers at JDK take it a step further. They often become end-users themselves. Their work for Burton Snowboards is a good example of how the JDK designers merge their lifestyles with their art. Snowboarding is probably the best recognized of the so-called extreme sports to emerge in the 1990s, even gaining status as an Olympic sport in the 1998 Winter Games. Its athletes are infamous for their reckless abandon and aggressiveness, and JDK's designers should know, since all three partners are snowboarders themselves, as are perhaps 80 percent of the studio's members. They deftly conveyed the snowboarder's attitude in Burton's designs, injecting the pieces with rapid action via lively images and kinetic typography—and humor. For example, one of their Burton advertisements poses the question, "Who the F—k is Terje?" (one of the sport's top athletes) with the offending letters disappearing into the bottom of a snowboard image. The result projects an assertive yet fun-loving attitude. The designers know instinctively how to appeal to this marketing-callous audience because they are intimately entwined with it.

The designers also recognize that their work impacts culture. *"Our audiences are mainly young people,"* says chief operating officer DAVID MENDELSON. *"We recognize that, whether it is a new product that we've designed or an advertisement, what we produce does affect their views. So we try to keep our social responsibility in mind whenever we design."*

Magic Hat Ale, *1994.*

Magic Hat Brewing Company is a small brewery in Burlington, Vermont, that is known for its odd specialty beers and distinct package graphics. JDK's design for this six-pack displays the brewery's strong identity in numerous color palettes that change with each beer flavor.

Mystic Eco-Adventures logo, *1995.*

The identity Jager Di Paola Kemp created for Mystic Eco-Adventures (a bicycle and bike equipment manufacturer) captures the culture of Barbados, where the company is headquartered, and its people, as well as the spirit of the sport.

Edward Mayer, *1996.*

The quirky, mystical forms of the artist were exploited to create a typographic interpretation of his work's flowing energy.

max kisman

Max Kisman Design, San Francisco, California

dutch defiance

In the early 1980s when NEVILLE BRODY was beginning to make waves in British design circles, MAX KISMAN was starting to make his mark in the Netherlands with his own forceful type-driven designs. Forgoing the Dutch tradition of type purity, Kisman was experimenting with typography and design marked by a raw freshness. *"The directness and visual power of primitive art and simple graphics—for example, a stop sign—always appealed to me,"* he explains. Newspaper cartoonists were another catalyst, both because of the crude nature of their drawings and their ability to reduce complex social issues to a clear, direct, accessible visual language.

Because he boasted a Radical attitude in one of the countries where design purity was born and still prevailed, Kisman's fame bordered on notoriety. He is acclaimed for his work in the early eighties as art director of the popular, but controversial, music magazine *Vinyl*, where he took great delight in defying the Dutch typographic legacy. His work became a major source of influence for other European designers stretching to move beyond the conservative look that most publications sported as they came out of the seventies. One item in particular stands out: Kisman redesigned *Vinyl's* logo, setting it in an expanded Garamond so it would be more accessible to readers and then, to communicate the magazine's contentious side, he turned the n upside down. A couple of years later, HUIB VAN KRIMPEN, considered the Dutch authority on typography, published the European design bible *The Book about the Making of Books*. It prominently featured the *Vinyl* logo—as an example of bad lettering.

That didn't bother Kisman. On the contrary, he considered it a compliment. He grew up in a family of creatives (his father was an illustrator and designer) and knows that innovation can breed criticism. His work has not gone unappreciated, however. He has earned many major European design awards, most notably the Audience Award of the Rotterdam Design Prize in 1995 and the revered H. M. Werkman Award in 1996.

Kisman graduated in 1977 from the illustration and design program at Amsterdam's Gerrit Rietveld Academy. His portfolio today includes samples of everything from exhibitions and books to postage stamps. In 1986, he cofounded *TYP/Typografisch Papier*, one of the first alternative magazines on typography and art. He was a digital

Vinyl, *1982.*

Kisman exploited the punk music scene's impudent colors, "ugly" typography, and garish imagery in Vinyl *magazine, which served as an open laboratory for many of his typographic and design experiments in the early 1980s.*

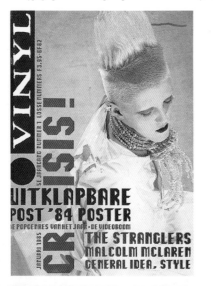

Paradiso Talenten Show, *1986.*

Kisman's series of posters for the Paradiso concert hall in Amsterdam along with his pioneering computer work for Language Technology *magazine thrust him into the forefront of Europe's digital design explosion.*

Stay Tuned, *1992.*

Kisman lived and worked in Barcelona from 1989 to 1992, designing revolutionary typefaces for FontShop International. He created this poster for FontShop's Berlin unit and Fuse *magazine.*

Euro bill, *1996.*

pioneer, and is noted for his work in the mid-1980s for *Language Technology* magazine and for the digital posters he created for Amsterdam's Paradiso concert hall. He has designed typefaces for FontShop International and *Fuse*, the experimental type magazine begun by NEVILLE BRODY. From 1991 to 1996 Kisman created animation for program announcements for the progressive Dutch television station VPRO, and he was associated with the graphic design collective WILD PLAKKEN. His varied experience has taught him that the design format itself can lead to the visual solution.

"The need to communicate will ensure that you try to reach a certain audience in a language they understand and appreciate," Kisman says, *"but language is a very lively, flexible, and changeable medium. Such change leads to differences in how we express ourselves visually and behaviorally."*

While Kisman's design process is driven by a classical objective—to reach the core of what a project should communicate and then relate the message simply—his nonconformist attitude assures that his work remains Radical. He may place an unexpected (and totally unrelated) image in an otherwise cleanly structured grid, such as the primitive skeletal icons he featured on a design proposal for the new Euro bill. The effect is more reminiscent of a playful JOAN MIRÓ painting than a serious monetary unit. And like Miró, who let intuition and impulse direct his work, Kisman often relies on spontaneity (in his case, brought on by deadlines) to guide him toward innovation. Finally, his typographic choices—he creates many of his own faces—project him into a progressive domain.

Kisman brought his talents to the United States in 1997 to serve as creative director of *Wired* (the innovative magazine that chronicles technological lifestyles) and its online affiliate, *Hotwired*, as well its short-lived broadcasting arm, Wired Television. A year later, he left *Wired* to open his own studio. The move to the States is a natural progression in Kisman's attempt to redefine his work, and it has enabled him to study firsthand the differences between European and American design attitudes.

Kisman admits that he has mellowed since making his name in Europe in the eighties, but he hasn't given up his quest for innovation. He hopes his explorations into the two design cultures will lead him into a new realm, one that will allow him another chance to make a positive contribution in design, this time on the American scene.

VPRO, *1996.*

This on-air station identity was among a series of graphics and animations
that earned Kisman the 1995 Rotterdam Design Prize's Audience Award and the
1996 H. M. Werkman Award.

Hotwired *icons, 1994.*

VPRO Web site, *1994.*

rebeca méndez

Rebeca Méndez Communication Design,
South Pasadena, California

shibumi

When REBECA MÉNDEZ was serving as art director of the Art Center College of Design, Pasadena, from 1992 to 1996, she was often told that her emotion-packed work was possible only because it was done for an educational audience and not *"for the real world."* She considers those who make such judgments victims of their own fear and mediocrity. *"Radical is all a matter of the openness or closedness of the viewer's mind,"* she says. *"It is unfortunate that Radical is associated with being an irresponsible communicator because most people I consider Radical are going beyond a limited* logos *[or analytical] communication to a fuller* logos *and* eros *[sensual] one."*

The Predisposed #2, 1992.

Méndez created this art installation using her official sixth-grade portrait, taken for the Secretariat of Public Education Systems in Mexico, and thirty-seven Idaho potatoes arranged in a typical student group formation. Méndez says the piece represents the boundaries by which we understand our place within society—systems of power and ordering that are so ingrained as to appear unquestionable and, to a large extent, form the lens through which we view the world.

Méndez's creations are remarkable for their sensuality, as well as their vitality and passion, all of which coexist within a precise structure, order, and system. Her designs communicate on many levels, frequently by playing off the tension that unfolds when classical structures operate in tandem with the unorthodox, such as in Art Center's 1995 catalog, on which she served as design director. When she conceived of the idea for the catalog in the spring of 1993, Méndez felt design was at a transitional point, standing before a threshold of changes brought on by new media and technology and led by the Internet. In fact, she felt the 1995 catalog might be the school's last printed one, so the idea of a book that was literally "broken" emerged. To suggest this brokenness while remaining a classically configured book, the catalog's pages are perforated horizontally. Inside, the perforation bisects sectional headlines that identify Art Center's areas of study, which gives rise to both a visual stimulus and a conceptual one. *"The perforation of the headlines creates hybrid words and opens our minds to the interdisciplinary and multidisciplinary environment at the college,"* Méndez explains. Text is randomly "distressed" throughout the book, while the question of what is an original image versus an exact replica is

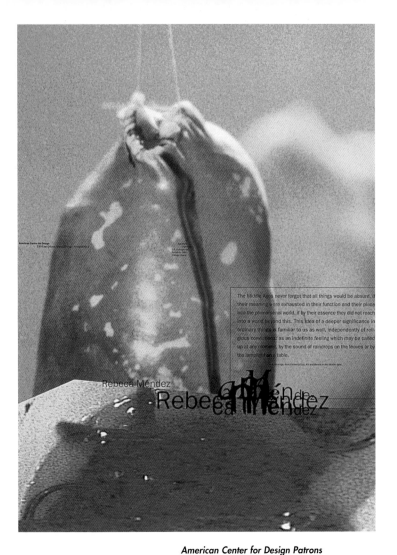

America Now, 500 Years Later, 1992.
This poster was part of an international invitational collection of forty posters commissioned by the second International Biennial of the Poster 1992, held in Mexico City. It explores identity issues, and the torso represents the individual in both its strength and vulnerability. Méndez attempted to dilute the celebration of Columbus's so-called "conquest" of the New World by reducing his ship to a decorative wallpaper element; the faint silhouette of the poodle serves as an example of how species ownership limits, traps, and distorts identity.

American Center for Design Patrons Night, *1995.*
This poster announced Méndez's exhibition and lecture at the American Center for Design in Chicago. The poster includes imagery from her fine art, videos, installations, and letterpress work.

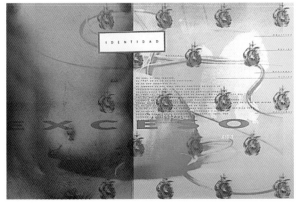

Cyber Stroke, *1996.*

Cyber Stroke is a twenty-second fine arts animation Méndez created for her partner, Adam Eeuwens, while he was living in Amsterdam. The animation consists of thirty-four dissolving frames, created on a Power Macintosh 7100/80 AV using Adobe Premier, Adobe Photoshop, and Sound Edit 16 software. Nine months after Cyber Stroke *was created, Eeuwens moved to Pasadena and the two became engaged.*

addressed by applying the continuous spatial and tonal variations of analog pictures to the discrete elements of digital images. The catalog's design reexamines the history of the college and of graphic design in general by *"seizing the transitional moment,"* Méndez says, and showcasing a culmination of recent design developments.

Méndez's affinity for creating work that projects multiple meanings is a result of her Mexican heritage, which celebrates coexistence and a hybrid way of life. *"I grew up knowing that one thing can be two or more things—like the planet Venus, which in the Mayan culture is considered both the Morning Star and the Evening Star. The Morning Star and the Evening Star exhibit totally opposing powers; still they are the same planet."* Mexico impacts her work in other ways, too. Her love of the sensual is an outgrowth of her treks through Mexico's jungles, slicing through the dense foliage with a machete. Her intrigue with typography is the by-product of endless hours spent studying Mayan glyphs at her father's side.

A critical point in the evolution of Méndez's work, however, occurred when she became completely disillusioned with graphic design, a career she had *"casually fallen into"* after being dissuaded from her original choices: mathematics, physics, and architecture. Three years after graduating from Art Center in 1989, already endowed with numerous awards from her peers, Méndez began to get the uneasy feeling that she had chosen *"a shallow and meaningless field of study."* So she returned to Art Center for an MFA in fine art, intending to abandon design altogether. But then something happened that would change her mind: she was offered a job

go2net identity and Web site, *1996–97.*
*Go2net, Inc., is an interactive technology
and media company that provides
proprietary and commodity information.
In creating its identity, Méndez used
elements from interactive media, such as
the windows found on the Web's search
engines where users type in key words
when doing a search. Go2net Web
site viewers are guided through its layers
by using signs on the surface pages
common to air navigation, then, once
they have entered the areas discussing specific topics, they are moved along by directional symbols common to freeway, street,
and pedestrian navigation.*

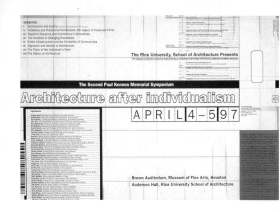

as the college's design director, a post that allowed her to attend classes tuition-free. Working for Art Center had an unexpected benefit: it restored her faith in design, helping her to realize that she was actually in control of her own creativity. It was up to her to select projects that didn't require leaving her brain and heart behind.

She also learned to set aside preconceived ideas and to view every subject emotionally as well as rationally, then to detect any mental filters that might stand in the way of a unique design solution. *"Most of the time people lack the courage to have a point of view and a voice, so they choose a very neutral—which comes from the word* neutered—*voice,"* Méndez remarks. She likens the process of creating a daring, personal design to that of archery. *"You lift the bow, place the arrow, then stretch the bow to its maximum,"* she explains. *"With single attention, yet an awareness of all, you point the arrow and, in* shibumi *[silent determination], let go. You cannot* not *communicate."*

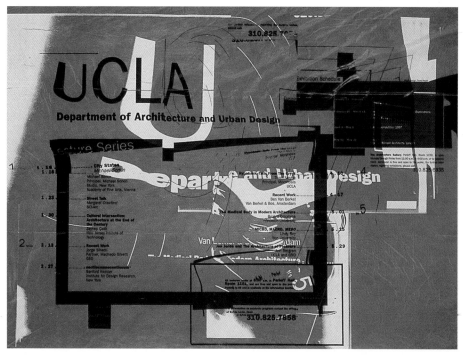

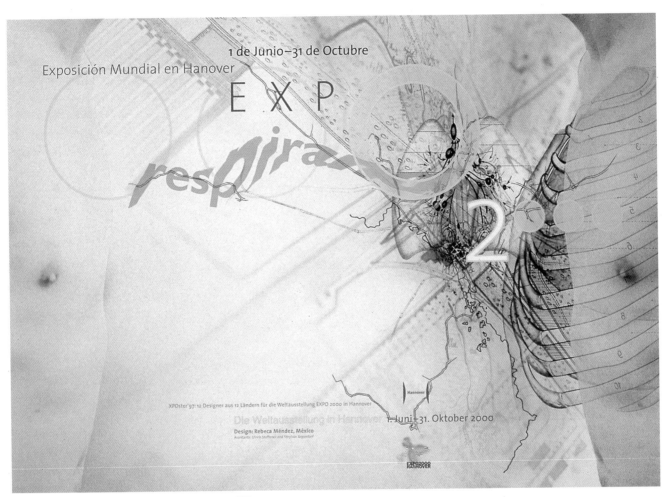

Within the image:

1 de Junio–31 de Octubre

Exposición Mundial en Hanover

E X P O

respira

2

XPOster'97: 12 Designer aus 12 Ländern für die Weltausstellung EXPO 2000 in Hannover

Die Weltausstellung in Hannover. 1. Juni–31. Oktober 2000

Design: Rebeca Méndez, México
Assistants: Ulrich Steffens and Stephan Angenfort

Hannover

EXPO2000
HANNOVER

Expo 2000, 1997.

Méndez was one of twelve international designers (she represented Mexico) who were asked to create posters demonstrating the spirit of World Expo 2000 in Hannover, Germany. The creative and production process lasted no more than three days: the first was devoted to exploring Hannover and its history, the second day to designing, and the third day to preparing the poster for printing. Méndez based her design on the significance of Hannover and on the anxiety brought on by the end of a millennium. "Continuity and acceptance of change is what I hope for in the new millennium," she notes. "In each breath, new air is inhaled and old air is exhaled: continuous exchange." The torsos on both ends of the poster both represent this exchange and resemble Hannover's logomark.

robynne raye
michael strassburger

Modern Dog Design Co., Seattle, Washington

loose as a goose

The type of clients MODERN DOG DESIGN CO. began working with when the studio was formed in the late 1980s is a major reason why it exists within the Radical realm today. Many were fringe theaters in the Seattle area, operating on minuscule budgets. The pay was lousy, but the payoff in artistic freedom was significant. In fact, the low budgets led to what partners ROBYNNE RAYE and MICHAEL STRASSBURGER refer to as their *"loose as a goose"* style of art. With no funds to hire freelance illustrators, Raye, Strassburger, and their design team (most notably, VITTORIO COSTARELLA and GEORGE ESTRADA) stretched beyond designing layouts to develop their own imagery. They never considered themselves illustrators, yet they came up with irreverent, often crudely executed characters and paired them with witty wordplay. The work often had the look of an old circus poster, featuring hand-lettering and bright, simple colors, inflicted with a heavy dose of kitsch. The offbeat results were a perfect match for the theaters' alternative offerings.

Although Modern Dog's work quickly attracted a following among the Northwest's young art community, it yielded few clients with money to spend. So in 1991, in a last-ditch effort to keep their studio from going under, Raye and Strassburger developed what has come to be known as the infamous "fur box." They filled ten portfolio boxes with work samples, goofy toys, and candy, then covered the boxes with fake brown fur. Wrapped around each box to hold it together was a dog collar bearing a tag with the studio's name and address. They mailed the boxes to a small but choice list of potential clients, including record companies and clothing manufacturers. The cost of each portfolio was significant—about eighty dollars—especially considering the studio was just shy of bankruptcy and Raye was contemplating shoplifting groceries to survive, she jokes. Yet the investment paid off in a big way: the fur boxes attracted a number of well-heeled clients—Capitol Records and Nike, among them—who were looking for just that sort of bizarre thinking to promote their youth-oriented products. While the promotion left many designers debating its artistic merits, they had to

Q1 Snowboards Squid and El Limbo, 1994.

Modern Dog's irreverence perfectly matches that of snowboard buyers. The image choices—Squid, created in Adobe Illustrator, and El Limbo, done by hand—were purely a matter of whim.

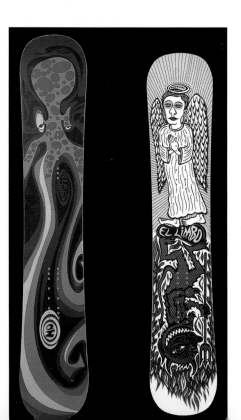

106

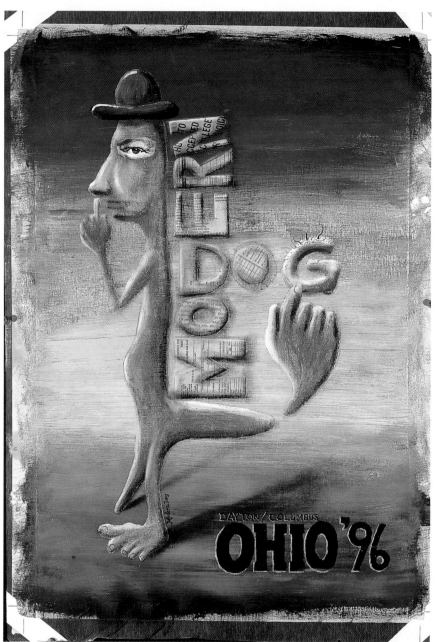

Ohio, *1996.*

Strassburger painted this image on the back of a
piece of Formica to announce the studio's presentation
to a design organization in Ohio.

K2 snowboard ad, *1996.*

This ad reflects the novelty of Tricky Glo, K2's "glow in the dark" snowboard.

Estrada created it in Adobe Illustrator and Adobe Photoshop.

admire Modern Dog's strong conceptual skills and, perhaps, even envy the designers' daring.

The designers at Modern Dog are accustomed to such odd twists and turns in their lives and their careers. Strassburger, for example, entered Western Washington University (WWU) on two high-school art scholarships, one of which he earned for his pencil drawing of a chopped-off head tied to a fence. He soon dropped out of school and went to work in a screenprinting shop. Unlike her classmate, Raye stayed at WWU long enough to earn a BA in graphic design. Still, she says, she has learned nearly everything she knows about the profession through trial and error; a full dumpster is the greatest inspiration for her work. The two formed their studio shortly after Raye graduated in the late 1980s, naming it after a dog groomer's sign. They were soon joined by designers George Estrada and Vittorio Costarella, who share the partners' idiosyncracies.

The Modern Dog team's humor and irreverent productions might disguise the fact that it's very serious about its work and about the design profession in general. Once, while in a debate with a group of their peers, they were told by designer and critic JEFFERY KEEDY that they were *on a fast track to nowhere,"* and he asked if they thought people would remember them in thirty years. Strassburger responded, *"What makes you think we want to be?"*

A place in history is not their prime goal. For now, it is enough of a challenge to break into new areas (like animation, film, and video) while keeping their studio solvent—and to keep sight of their "loose as a goose" attitude and style.

Syracuse University Presents, 1997.

*When Modern Dog was asked to design a poster for its speaking engagement at
Syracuse University, Raye was inspired by circus broadsides to create this poster. It represents
how she views Modern Dog's presentation style—like a circus freak show.*

Third Annual Rainy States Film Festival, *1997.*

*The "rough" look of Costarella's handcrafted illustration
is intended to represent the independent filmmakers who
participate in this festival.*

Feedback, *1996.*

*This newsletter is for music lovers. Shown are the front and back
covers from the winter 1996 issue. Bands of color and type
above and below the cover image, as well as the blue used to lend
interest to the static photo image, punch up the cover.*

somi kim
lisa nugent
susan parr

ReVerb, Los Angeles, California

intriguing nuances

REVERB, which was formed in 1990 and is led today by partners and creative directors SOMI KIM, LISA NUGENT, and SUSAN PARR, is one group among the Radicals that has earned its due respect. Featured in a 1996 *Los Angeles Times* article ("Graphic Design Gets a Life," September 5) and voted the following year as one of *ID* magazine's "Top 40" West Coast design firms, the studio is noted for its dynamic visual vocabulary output in print, on-line, and for television. The designers' fascination with modernistic forms and dramatic typography dominates much of their work, often merged in colorful layers of imagery and text. The stimulating results have earned them a list of well-known clients (Nike, MTV, Netscape, the Metropolitan Transit Authority of Los Angeles, the Asian Society, and so on) whose tastes run the gamut from Baroque to classical, from "corporate corporate" to corporate hip.

Now Time, *1994.*

ReVerb created the logo and cover of the premiere issue of this alternative magazine that showcased new art, new writing, and popular culture. The logo incorporates old and new technologies (the word Time *was blurred manually on a photocopier) and includes a nod to vernacular and the ubiquitous stop sign, seen in the o of* Now. *The back cover photograph, by Anthony Cook, captures a lunar eclipse that took place when the magazine was coming together.*

Their work is mostly media-driven, *"whether next, new, thirty minutes ago, historic, or anachronistic,"* Kim notes. *"We are influenced by spin doctors, yarn spinners, reporters, documentarians, artists of all kinds. The following terms represent different aspects of our work: think tank, workshop, image consultants, creative producers, design studio. Our consistent methodology is to use language and observation to create or identify stories and give them visual expression."*

Collaborating in an almost *"exquisite corpse"* approach—in which participants build off each other's work by independently adding their input and then passing it on to the next team member—often leads them to their imaginative ends and, as such, is a major part of their creative process. A poster they developed for the launch of an interactive telecommunications device called PowerPhone is a good example. The designers split up into two teams to create the poster, with the first fashioning what they called a *"sea of chaos"* as a metaphor for existing telecommunications technology for the

110

PowerPhone poster, *1997.*

"Championing the Verb" title page and spread, 1996.

Metropolis *magazine featured ReVerb in its "By Design" column in the article "Championing the Verb" by Véronique Vienne (July/August 1996). ReVerb was asked to design the first three pages of the article to demonstrate its work process. In this spread, ReVerb posited a number of questions about how a logo might act, then catalogued the results of the questions on the spread, along with inspirational source material in outlined boxes. The bottom part of the spread charts the "magazine landscape" over a pinhole photograph commissioned from Tres Parsons.*

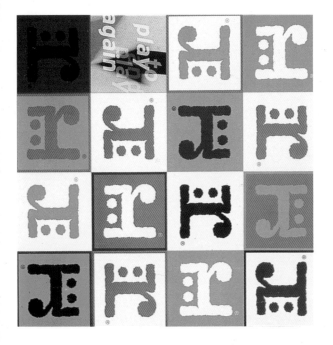

Reprise Records, 1994–96.

ReVerb's strategy for reinvigorating the identity of Reprise Records was to recast historic elements from the company's past, including the motto "To Play and Play Again." The logo had been cleaned up in the 1980s; ReVerb moved it more toward the original, craggier mark used in the 1960s by commissioning typographer Gino Lee to redraw it. ReVerb completed the identity by developing a flexible color palette and a playful application of the logo to different packaging and stationery pieces.

poster's background. They created their "sea" by scanning images and photographs into an Adobe Photoshop file and coloring them in muted reds and browns. Simultaneously, the second team was at work on digitally creating a PowerPhone image to present a *"window of simple sophistication,"* used as a visual metaphor for the product's new technology. The two files were then merged to *"represent two worlds flowing together,"* according to the designers.

Another design they created for a 1996 article on their work called "Championing the Verb," which ran in *Metropolis* magazine (July/August issue), offers insight into how concept affects their design process. The magazine's editors asked ReVerb to develop a hypothetical redesign of its banner. The designers began by questioning the *Metropolis* staff about how they saw their place in the *"magazine landscape."* The word catalyst came up, and the ReVerb designers fixed on it, sketching, inking, and incorporating it into their mock cover design along with a photo of a spinning top. ReVerb next developed a set of questions to address in the article centering on how a logo might "act"—things such as *"How would the logo look if it were viewed through a lens?"* *"What if it spun like a top?"* and *"What if the logo were an artifact?"* Then they answered the questions visually and provided examples of inspirational sources.

Aside from their creative talents, the studio offers clients another asset: their own heterogeneity, which makes them sensitive to other cultures and the frequent inadequacy of market research. The particular mix of individuals at ReVerb is culturally diverse both nationally and internationally, with two native southern Californians and the balance hailing variously from the Pacific Northwest, the Midwest, the Southeast, the Northeast, Germany, and Hong Kong. *"We collectively consider appropriate visual 'dialects' when approaching each project,"* remarks Kim, *"and are possibly more aware of the pitfalls of superficial cultural sampling because of our location in the midst of a hype-driven, ethnically diverse, American-Californian decentered urban center."*

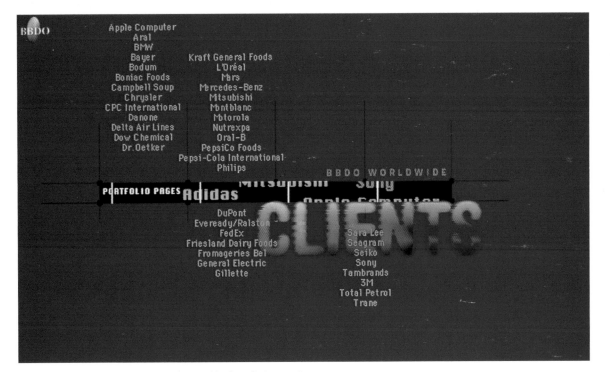

BBDO Worldwide Web site, *1996.*

BBDO Worldwide wanted its Web site to be "corporate hip"—new-looking without transgressing the advertising agency's corporate standards. This page shows one of a number of splash screens that lead to different contents within the site. The overall design strategy was to minimally use available technology for maximum effect: hence the narrow Shockwave window that contains the client roster, set in a tweaked version of a computer standard typeface, used as a cursor-responsive, dynamic event.

CalArts Bulletin, *1996.*

Three consecutive bulletins for the California Institute of the Arts were produced by ReVerb in collaboration with Heavy Meta, San Francisco. Each new bulletin was designed in reaction to its predecessor. For example, only one type family (Schadow) was used throughout the third bulletin (shown), a marked change from the second, which featured seven.

The partners also give credit to their design teachers for their success, particularly for steeping them in the basics of their art and then encouraging them to search for better ways to communicate. Kim graduated from Harvard in 1984 with a degree in visual and environmental studies, followed by an MFA in graphic design from CalArts in 1989. Nugent began her education in illustration, earning a degree in 1981 from California State University Long Beach before entering Yale's Summer Program in 1985 and then earning an MFA in design from CalArts in 1988. Parr took classes in journalism and fine arts at the University of Oregon and Pacific Northwest College of Art, respectively, before being awarded a BFA in graphic design from Parsons School of Design in 1986.

They find it challenging to keep producing fresh work and to live up to their professors' exhortations. *"There's so much recycling and sampling and remixing in design that just focusing your eyes can make you a 'follower,'"* Kim remarks.

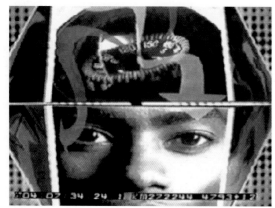

Excite, Are You Experienced, *1996.*

ReVerb worked closely with director Jeffrey Plansker (Propaganda Films) and ad agency Foote Cone Belding (San Francisco) to develop the look of the thirty-second broadcast spot for Excite, an Internet search engine. Classic Blue Note album covers were among the "swipes" used as a springboard to other ideas. After designing a palette of colors and elements for the different iterations of the spot, ReVerb took stills from live-action footage, manipulated them, added graphic elements, and output the frames as oversized Iris prints. These prints were actually built onto a polyhedron whose top and bottom halves would independently rotate (with a soundtrack by Jimi Hendrix) and stop with different top/bottom combinations. Transition animation showing the search engine in use and a psychedelic hand/eye were also provided by ReVerb.

Language As Creation, *1999.*

These introductory spreads for Wired *magazine sprang from the concept that language itself is a code that creates.*

Avalon Hotel identity and signage, *1999.*

The image and identity design of the former Beverly Carlton Hotel integrates ReVerb's effort to articulate a memorable personality that combines echoes of the hotel's mid-century design roots (by Alvin Lustig) with a contemporary interpretation of California patio lifestyle.

carlos segura

Segura, Inc. and [T-26], Chicago, Illinois

a progeny of his time

To say that CARLOS SEGURA's iconoclastic approach to design evokes an emotional response from viewers is to put it mildly. Once he was invited to an informal after-hours session at a conference to discuss the program he had created for the event, since some attendees were finding the booklet hard to read. To Segura's amazement, a ballroom of bellicose critics showed up, ready for battle. Before the evening was over he had been called everything from "hostile" to "communist." Even more startling, it was the 1993 *HOW* Design Conference and the critics were his peers. Segura maintained his composure throughout, rationally explaining his simple design philosophy: communication that doesn't take a chance doesn't have a chance. Just a few years later, that attitude has helped him earn numerous awards and clients.

HOW *Design Conference program, 1993.*

Segura's technique is emotionally driven, much of it the result of spontaneous impulse. *"I approach communication pretty much the way I approach my career,"* he says. *"It's just from the gut."* Perhaps that is why he can easily switch gears, working within a clearly defined grid for one type catalog, while for another allowing the typeface itself to dictate each page's design posture. Segura likes to combine the old with the new— such as using computer-generated illustrations enhanced by lush colors along with letterpress printed on an industrial paper for a surprising coup de grâce. He gives new life to design by indiscriminately mixing earthy hues and corporeal patterns, evocative of Egyptian hieroglyphics, with voluptuous letterforms and layered words. His work is charged by an eclectic array of digitized typefaces (many his own creations) whose design conveys the message as lucidly as the words. No design element injects more personality than type, he believes; a project's attitude can be altered simply by changing the font. Legibility is often a non-issue. Instead, a sensual tactility and raw, almost erotic passion is the crux.

Segura is a musician at heart whose original ambition was to become a sound editor. With no formal design training per se, he has no qualms about breaking design's sacred rules. Instead, he cut his design teeth in the early seventies creating flyers for a disco band in Miami in which he served as drummer and promotions

creative vision

HOW The 1993 HOW DESIGN CONFERENCE on Business and The Creative Process. April 25th thru 28th, 1993. The Westin Hotel, Chicago, Illinois.

116

Segura identity, 1992.

Blackbox, 1995.

Segura's ability to relate to Gen-X youth attracts many music-
related clients. This limited-edition CD provides a historical
overview of WaxTrax! Records' thirteen years. WaxTrax! promotes
industrial music, a hard-core, heavy-metal sound. Segura's caustic
visuals complement the label's guttural strains.

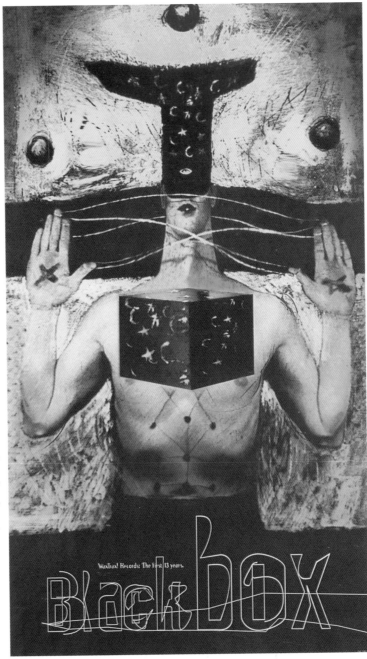

The Alternative Pick, *1996.*

The Alternative Pick is a national sourcebook of music industry talents. Each year, one of design's most innovative practitioners is asked to create the book, raising it from mere sourcebook to valued inspiration. Segura's book and campaign were based on the theme "an organic celebration of life."

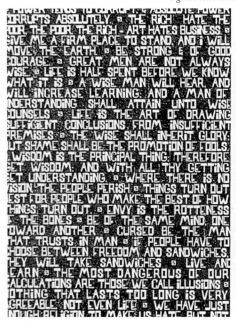

Q101 invitation, *1996.*

Chicago radio station Q101 invites artists to play their current hits on the air, then it releases an annual CD of their performances. This invitation to the station's Christmas party for media buyers is a take-off on that CD. The main door prize was a free trip to Milan to see the Red Hot Chili Peppers, one of the groups featured on the 1996 CD.

AgfaType, Idea catalog, 1995.
AgfaType of Chicago wanted a catalog
with "inspiration, direction, and design
focus built into the concept." So twelve
prominent Chicago-based designers, illus-
trators, and photographers created a piece
of art from their favorite typeface, then
Segura compiled the work into the cata-
log using his favorite design tools—Adobe
Photoshop and letterpress.

DJ Razorface CD, *1999.*

This CD provided an unrestrained outlet for Segura's artistic inclinations, since it was for his own band, on his Thickface Records label. A throwback to Segura's disco days, the group plays club dance music.

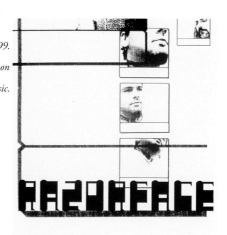

fig. 20 Sunflower Landscape

Maramara catalog, *1996.*

Segura's work for Maramara, a cutting-edge milliner, demonstrates the diversity of clients the Radical look attracts. This catalog went out to exclusive retailers.

manager. His first "real" design job came a few years later, fashioning return addresses and privacy patterns for bank envelopes. This, in turn, led to a dozen years designing in ad agencies. But Segura became increasingly frustrated with the advertising environment and what he perceived as a lack of concern for good design. When his dream job as art director at an ad agency in Japan fell through, he knew it was time for a change. In 1980 Segura moved to Chicago and found a design job at a studio. (True to his impulsive nature, he chose that city simply because he liked the way its name sounds.) Eleven years later, he decided to strike out on his own, and he opened Segura Inc. He expanded his firm in 1994 to include [T-26], a type foundry that offers an array of novel fonts invented by some of today's most eccentric typographers.

His *Saturday Night Fever* days are long gone, but music still manifests itself throughout Segura's work. No person serves as his mentor or inspiration; music injects the soul. Record stores are his never-ending source of inspiration. To him, they are like modern art galleries where the latest trends in everything from typography and photography to packaging, layout, special effects, and illustration can be discovered.

And, of course, there is the impact of the computer. Segura's first was an Apple that he bought just because he liked how it looked. It sat in his living room for two months before he opened it, but once he did he never glanced back. Unlike those who maintain the computer is merely another design tool, Segura admits he would be crippled without it. Once he was asked how the computer affects his work, and the designer candidly replied that it *is* his work. *"I don't even know how to draw and I wouldn't be in this business without it,"* Segura says. *"I'm a progeny of our time."*

XXX Snowboards, *1996.*

This catalog provides a calendar, trip chart, tips on snowboard ethics, 800 numbers to call for snowboard information, and more. In effect, it is a snowboarder's guidebook, which elevates it to "keeper" status.

glenn mitsui
jesse doquilo
randy lim

Studio MD, Seattle, Washington

out of the comfort zone

The quest for individuality can take many paths. In STUDIO MD's case, it ended in illustration for two of the firm's three partners. They began as designers, but to fulfill their clients' imaging needs (especially those with limited budgets) both GLENN MITSUI and JESSE DOQUILO began creating their own illustrations. They soon discovered that illustrating honed their conceptual prowess and enhanced their storytelling ability. It also helped them develop a unique perspective and style that integrates color, geometric shapes, and multilayered images in compositions that often cross the line between commercial and personal art. Illustration also helped the studio lure a number of clients it might not have attracted through design alone. K2, Proflex Bikes, *Atlantic Monthly*, *Rolling Stone*, *Sierra On-Line*, Chateau Ste. Michelle winery, and McCann-Erickson Advertising are just a few of the diverse companies that use the studio's services. *"Illustration allows us to go places where we wouldn't be able to go if we were just a design firm,"* remarks Doquilo.

Love on a Wall, *1997.*

One of a series of nine images created for Aeino Cosmetics, Love on a Wall offers Mitsui's interpretation of how memory degrades. The piece functions on many levels and offers diverse emotional assessments.

All three partners are from Seattle and studied design at area schools. RANDY LIM (who focuses purely on design work) and Doquilo earned degrees from the University of Washington (UW), while Mitsui *"stumbled through"* a community college. At the time, UW was *"a very, very Swiss program, with a heavy use of grids and Times Roman,"* Doquilo recalls. That methodology is still deeply rooted in him, but now he builds off that base using as inspiration his experiences traveling, meeting people, visiting museums, and studying the work of those creatives *"who live and breathe art,"* especially abstract painters and the Surrealists, German printmakers, and collagists. *"That influence has allowed me to have a looser, open approach to my computer collage style for actual projects,"* Doquilo says.

Doquilo, the son of Filipino immigrants, has recently begun to explore his heritage and incorporate it into his fine art pieces. One piece, *Influence*, was produced after his first trip to the Philippines, which he recalls as an *"an intense cultural overload,*

This image is one in a series of nine that Doquilo created while searching for a new style of illustration.

He devoted three weeks to developing what he now calls his Visual DJ style, a layered look

featuring spontaneous colors and imagery taken from clip art, typography, photography, paintings, and

found objects. He plays off his mistakes rather than hides them, and textural subtleties fill every inch of the

piece. Doquilo grew up with the attitude that "less is more"; in this illustrative style, "more is busier."

meeting fifty relatives for the first time." The piece was exhibited in a 1998 show on Filipino artists at Seattle's Wing Luke Asian Museum. It was created from randomly selected images mixed with others that have a highly personal meaning for Doquilo, forming abstract shapes and unique juxtapositions. For instance, a combination of old photos of his parents is *"a tribute to the values that they instilled in me and their sacrifices"* ; the human form (a photo of a sculpture) represents Doquilo's soul under his mother's watchful eye; random textures and colors abstractly represent memories from his life's experiences. The result is a personal study of spontaneous color, shapes, and imagery.

Mitsui's creative process is also affected by his rich cultural heritage. His earliest influences were the great Japanese designers. Trips to Tokyo likewise energize him, but mostly it is the childhood memories of growing up as a Japanese American that affect him today. *"My grandparents and parents were interned in concentration camps during World War II because of their race,"* he remarks. *"The hardships they had to endure, what they sacrificed to make sure I succeeded, are driving forces in my determination to keep on."*

Mitsui also draws inspiration from the Seattle area's youths, who learn about design by working in Studio MD as part of a mentoring program that he helped found. *"The fearless abandon they exhibit and the joy of creating are things which I have to remind myself daily to remember,"* he notes. *"One example of how children have influenced my work is the poster image for MacWorld Tokyo. The main image was influenced by the paintings of a snowman by my little girl's first grade class. Granted, my interpretation came out looking mean and twisted, but I still had a lot of fun doing it."*

Another major catalyst for Mitsui was his first job *"at the Boeing School of Design."* He started out at the aeronautics manufacturer by applying arrows to milestone charts with Chart Pak tape before working his way up to technical illustrator, drawing nuts and bolts and scaffolding. Finally, he advanced to the computer graphics department to work on slide shows, where he learned how to draw on the computer by translating squares, circles, and lines into the system. The boring, mundane existence drove

The Year 2000, *1997.*

Doquilo's first stab at a commercial application for his Visual DJ style was this illustration, created for an InfoWorld *article on how the change to the year 2000 is expected to wreak havoc on computers. Doquilo focused on systems managers' emotions as they approach this dilemma, rather than relying on computer references, to make a point. The layering and randomness of the imagery add to the chaotic feel of this intentionally busy piece.*

Discovery, *1997.*

This image for Discovery *magazine accompanies an article on new advances in Web technology that enhance the online experience. Mitsui wanted to experiment with different perspectives to reflect the new, entertaining devices offered by the Web. The sculptural pieces illustrate the five senses.*

Resolution Technologies packaging, *1996.*

Studio MD's identity for this software, which allows interactive visualization and navigation of very large three-dimensional images, reflects the product's gamelike qualities while giving it a unique look.

Mitsui to develop an unexpected asset: the courage to take chances. He realized that to avoid a life of repetitive, nonchallenging work, he would have to climb out of his comfort zone and go out on a limb, engaging in innovative creations that would attract like-minded clients.

He and his studio partners live by that creed today, which drives them in their ongoing creative evolution. *"It's kind of like getting on a merry-go-round that moves,"* Mitsui explains. *"You have these different brass rings all over the place that you grasp for. You must keep taking risks in your style, and much of that involves not being afraid to fail. We fall flat on our faces a lot, but we're supportive of each other and we keep trying."*

Urban Man, Chipman, FaceMan, *1997.*

This series of illustrations was born from Mitsui's desire to explore the power of a black line. The simple approach was inspired by the work of artists Keith Haring and Jauqin Torres Garcia, and by various rock petroglyphs. Adding dimension and the Spirograph elements brings out a playfulness.

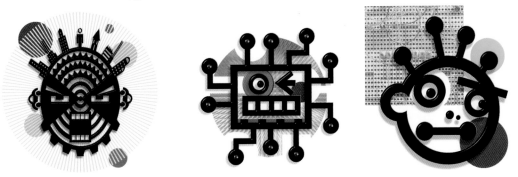

paul sych

Faith, Toronto, Canada

improvise

PAUL SYCH's work is a collision of the visually lyrical and the blatantly technical that's infused with a pop-art-gone-digital charisma. Loud colors, protracted typography, and robust forms prevail. Sych considers his designs artistic improvisations, in the same way that, as a jazz musician, he might get caught up in the heated energy of a jam session and refashion a classic favorite into a uniquely personal rendition. Ultimately, the song becomes an intermingling of the composer's and the musician's voices. In the same manner, Sych takes fonts, colors, and shapes and mixes them together in his own way to create a new visual language.

Design is all about curiosity, enchantment, and the unknown, Sych says. Having found these elements in his music, he now seeks to uncover them in his design work. Sych has been equally drawn to the two artistic forms since his student days, when he was simultaneously enrolled in Ontario College of Art's design curriculum and York University's esteemed jazz program. After graduating in 1978, he set aside his design aspirations for a career in music, playing in bands for seven years. He managed a tuxedo shop during the day to make ends meet. Then his wife talked him into interviewing for a job at a Toronto typesetting house, and he ended up as its delivery person, paste-up artist, and film and plate maker. It wasn't long before the company went bankrupt—but it was long enough to rekindle Sych's interest in design.

He found a new job as a magazine layout artist for a printer, where he first began to experiment with headline type, expanding it and distorting it—anything to draw the reader in. Eventually, Sych's typographic talents landed him a position at LOUIS FISHAUF's internationally recognized design studio REACTOR, where Sych says he came of age. Fishauf was a pioneer in computer-produced design, but Sych credits him with much more than introducing him to technology's artistic potential. Fishauf taught Sych to look beyond design annuals and to take note of what was happening around him for inspiration.

While most of his colleagues shied away from Reactor's point-of-purchase projects, many of which were created for major retailers, Sych found great enjoyment working on them. He considered such projects true design challenges whose solutions centered almost

***Don't Look at It, Look to It,** 1996.*
Sych was working as creative director on a music magazine when he received a letter from a designer criticizing him for Wit, a font he had created for the magazine, which was inspired by early-twentieth-century design legend Kurt Schwitters. Sych remarked, "This designer was particularly nasty—he said the typeface Dom Casual would have been much better. So I did this poster and sent it to him. I never heard from him again."

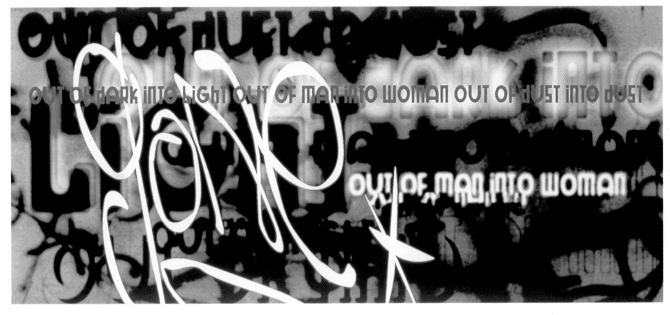

Gone, *1993.*

Does unity between the sexes truly exist? This 4-by-8-foot mural Sych created,

and which hangs in the Faith studio, offers his viewpoint.

Jesus Saves, *1996.*

This poster promotes a font Sych created called U.S. that lampoons the popularity of America's corporate

icons and their takeover of many previously sacred entities, such as the Olympics.

The Population Cannot Ignore the Truth, *1996.*

This single-page illustration was created for a 10-by-12 inch booklet promoting Sych's illustrations. The image was also used in a ten-minute animated spot that followed the release of the booklet.

exclusively on type. They put his creative skills to the test as he searched for new ways to grab shoppers' attention in a matter of seconds. Sych excelled at his work. Eventually, he felt that he needed to move beyond designing for Reactor and begin developing his own design vernacular. Faith, a studio he formed in late 1990, is the result.

Since establishing Faith, Sych has accumulated a list of clients that includes nearly every major advertising agency in Canada, and he has contributed to campaigns for such companies as McDonald's, General Motors, and Coca-Cola. He also has entered the video market, creating type design and images for a music television station and graphics for a rock video. Whatever the format, Sych's distinct style comes through. He believes the singularity of his work is, simply, a consequence of believing in oneself. *"I've created something that, in my heart, is unique, and belongs to me only,"* he says. *"It's almost like I went to Las Vegas, bet on myself against all odds, then rolled the dice."*

Much of Sych's work today still hinges on typography. He creates many of his own faces—something that is not surprising considering that his prime influences are NEVILLE BRODY and Toronto's profusion of signage—and he is gaining an international reputation for his work. Noted typeface designer ED CLEARY (owner of the type house FontShop Canada) has compared Sych's avant-garde typefaces and type-driven imagery to Brody's, adding that just as the British designer has had to continually evolve his work to stay ahead of imitators, Sych will likely have to do the same. RICK VALICENTI is another admirer, calling Sych's designs *"strong, powerful, and direct in a pop sense."*

Music also remains a major factor in his life, both as a metaphor and an art; at night, look for him in a Toronto jazz club playing guitar with the Paul Sych Trio. But when he's at work, he thinks of design like a musical improvisation. Just as a soloist improvises while retaining a sense of harmony and rhythm, Sych believes that certain design conventions will always prevail. These include a strong sense of color, form, and most of all, typographic intellect. At the same time, just as a wrong note in a jazz composition can become the cornerstone of an entirely new song, he's always open to a design imperfection that might lead the way to a new visual approach.

What If?, *1997.*

Created for Experimental Typography, *a 1998 design book by Rob Carter, this image grapples with the question of what artists can achieve and their uncertainty over what will happen when they sit down to create.*

Faith sweater, *1997.*

Sych's bold designs translate well to products, as seen in this sweater marketed under the Faith label. Texture gives his sweaters a digitized, bit-mapped look. A Faith jewelry line includes pins, necklaces, rings, and key chains.

dana arnett, robert vogele
james koval, curt schreiber
ken schmidt

VSA Partners, Chicago, Illinois

subtle subversives

Some may be surprised to discover the work of VSA PARTNERS included in a collection of Radical artists. Yet the firm's designers definitely number among them. Their subversive nature merely exerts itself in subtle ways: a paperless, video docu-comedy on the rise and fall of an art director is developed as a paper promotion. A Type Director's Club conference, focusing on cutting-edge multimedia design and typography, is announced with a poster that has the look and feel of something produced by a low-tech cartoon artist. Set against a baby blue background is a naive, bad-to-the-point-of-kinky illustration of a stereotypical, pipe-smoking ad agency boss who is admonishing his staff for using sophisticated computer equipment to draw pictures of naked women. The VSA team named this poster, to even further poke fun at the whole idea of technology, Techweenie.

As do many of the firm's works, this seemingly simple poster traverses multiple levels of complex issues. It offers a fitting parody of what design has become—a profession caught up in technology to a point that often overshadows creativity—and it makes a satirical comment on sexism in the industry. Such comedy plays a major role in defining VSA's Radical persona. The designers lean toward British satire, which relies strongly on wordplay, and they will search for two lines of copy and a photo that are as powerful as something others might spend four weeks trying to accomplish with Adobe Photoshop. *"When you are pushing for your work to rise above a conventional level, writing has to be integral,"* partner DANA ARNETT remarks. Bold ideas, then, become the core of their design strategy rather than visual subterfuge.

VSA's Radical originality is also a product of application. Innovation is achieved via composition and the manner in which the designers position traditional elements in nontraditional ways. One Harley-Davidson project provides a strong example of when personality and character contradict classical conventions. The piece, a poster announcing a

Techweenie, 1996.

A technology-based conference has the potential to sound a bit dry. Unexpected colors and a low-tech approach, in conjunction with a controversial statement on the front of this poster, announced that this one would be anything but dull.

Eaglethon poster, 1996.

Smoking Popes, Destination Failure *packaging,* *1997.*

motorcycle event Harley sponsored, features a historically styled painting of an All-American rider, rather than the unkempt, tough-as-nails Hell's Angel–type character most associate with a Harley hog.

Creative talents such as designer TIBOR KALMAN, who emphasizes content over visual shock, provide the VSA team with inspiration. The late SAUL BASS, whom the designers admire for his resistance to confinement and his willingness to explore new arenas, is especially motivating to them. *"I try to walk in those steps, but they're really big ones,"* Arnett says. Shortly before he died, Bass told Arnett something the designer says he will never forget. *"There's one difference between filmmakers and designers,"* Bass said. *"Good filmmakers understand how important the story is, while designers tend to become mesmerized by how it looks and how it works visually."* This advice drives the studio's work today.

Ministry, Filth Pig *CD package,* *1996.*
This CD's artwork illustrates the concepts behind the band's songs.
It also portrays the political climate of America through images depicting
the right-wing movement and its effect on the country's citizens.

132

Luna, Bella Luna, 1997.

When Arnett saw Paul Elledge's photographs of Versale, Italy, he was immediately struck by their spirit, elegance, and simplicity. He strove to evoke those feelings with the book's design.

martin venezky

Appetite Engineers, San Francisco, California

intuitive revelations

Can a single design ever be universal, created in a manner so that every individual will read it exactly the same? Not without being bland or cliché, MARTIN VENEZKY believes. For that reason, the designer abhors Corporate America's reverence for market research. Research has made some companies much money, he concedes, but in the long run it has had a disastrous side effect. It has virtually destroyed the country's once remarkable popular culture by leading many to believe that what is good for one project is likewise good for the next. In effect, he blames market research for the cookie-cutter look of much of today's design.

Theater Zeebelt, 1993.

This is one in a series of posters Venezky created for Theater Zeebelt, an ongoing promotional and informational project from Studio Dumbar. He created the poster by screenprinting the images over the same four-color offset base.

When seeking solutions for his own clients' creative challenges, Venezky prefers intuitive revelation over numbers-driven, formulaic schemes. *"I try not to repeat what an audience is used to seeing,"* Venezky notes, *"but to seduce them into a new way of thinking."* Flowing letterforms mingle among, or sometimes even seem to caress, unexpected, striking images, many of which are taken from Venezky's expansive collection of graphic design ephemera or his own photography. Luminous colors lend an almost romantic, sentimental undertone to the designer's powerful digital vernacular. His editorial work, most notably that done for *Speak*, an art, music, film, and fiction magazine, can do an abrupt about-face within a single issue. A chaotic, grid-busting spectacular of text blocks, imagery, and hues is stamped across one spread. Turn the page to the next spread and Venezky exhibits a subdued restraint that effectively melds the article's design with the creations of the writer and photographer. *"After all,"* he reasons, *"the magazine is not about me, but about the articles. I don't try to hide, but I don't choose to trample either."*

Venezky's love of graphic design and letterforms began when he was very young. His uncle, a calligrapher and cartographer, would bring him gifts of Speedball pens and type catalogs. In 1979, Venezky graduated from Dartmouth College (New Hampshire) with a degree in fine arts. Although Dartmouth did not then offer graphic design courses, one of Venezky's professors recognized a strong

Red River, *1993.*

Red River *is one of several collages in "Notes on the West," done while Venezky was a Cranbrook*

student. It was created on a color photocopier from photographs and photostats.

Magic Johnson, George Bush, *1992.*

Venezky created this poster while a student at Cranbrook as a spontaneous response to basketball

player Magic Johnson's press conference and President Bush's appointment of him to the Presidential

Commission on AIDS. Venezky began on the computer, then turned to conventional design

methods for its completion, cutting and reworking the type using an X-Acto knife on laser output.

135

Stand by Your Man, *1992.*

Venezky's personal photography

often appears in his designs, as seen

in this piece for Ray Gun.

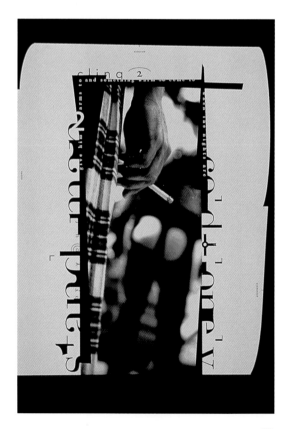

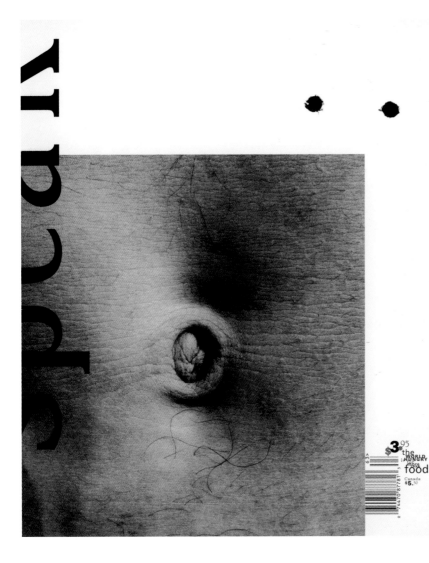

Speak, *1996–98.*

Speak *has evolved into a magazine covering art, fiction, and film, along with fashion and music. Venezky's designs, which have evolved, too, are driven by the magazine's youthful, alternative-minded audience. Shown are the fall 1996 cover (left) and the July 1998 cover (issue 10), in which* Speak's *new logo and smaller format debuted.*

CCAC card, *1995.*

This card, a collaboration with Lucille Tenazas, represents a search for how to turn mundane objects into intriguing possibilities. The poem offers a "secret message" to Venezky's students at California College of Arts and Crafts on listening to other designers discuss their work.

Reebok Exhibit, *1998.*

Venezky created this tradeshow exhibit and graphics for Reebok International using a language based on athletic motion and performance rather than the idea of athletes as superstars or shoes as a lifestyle, which was how most sports shoes were being marketed in the 1990s.

Bordertown, *1997.*

design sensibility in his work. So he helped Venezky secure a post at the Hopkins Center Design Studio, which was responsible for creating posters for the college's cultural events. Here Venezky learned *"formal"* design skills while on the job. He spent the next dozen years working in studios until entering Cranbrook Academy of Art in pursuit of an MFA. Like many others who have passed

Venezky and design assistant Geoff Kaplan collaborated closely with writer Barry Gifford and photographer David Perry in developing the narrative for this book about towns along the United States and Mexico border. The two designers were allowed to select text passages and drawings from Gifford's notes, and their own choices from Perry's collection of photographs, which, in effect, makes them quasiauthors of the book.

through Cranbrook's doors, Venezky found that the school's strong conceptual focus changed the entire manner in which he approached his work. He developed new ways of seeing, thinking, and creating. Venezky graduated from skilled technician to cerebral pioneer.

In Venezky's opinion, deliberation and continual questioning keep a designer's work fresh. *"If you have never learned to think about the world and develop your ideas and forms from your thoughts,"* he says, *"you will always be applying a current style—someone else's—to whatever information you are given. That style will always be changing and you will always be running to catch up. However, if you can learn to look at and question the world, extract a formal vocabulary from your topic and your imagination, and develop your own voice from your unique way of thinking, then you can step aside from the mad rush."*

david ellis
andrew altmann
patrick morrissey

Why Not Associates, London, England

the entertainers

A reviewer once described the introduction WHY NOT ASSOCIATES created for design editor RICK POYNOR's book *Typography Now: The Next Wave* (Booth-Clibborn Editions, 1991) as *"unreadable."* The introduction is an articulate demonstration of what Why Not partner ANDREW ALTMANN means when he says the studio frequently employs *"type as entertainment."* The title page is turned on its side; column placement and widths vary at whim; random words and phrases are linked via spastic lines; and other text is highlighted with bright colors and jagged backdrops and by setting it in varying fonts, styles, and sizes. At times, a casually selected sentence is stretched across the book's gutter, holding the reader's eye hostage and forcing it to the opposite page. In spite of the criticism, there is a sense of control, a logical flow from one page to the next. Even in its wildest manifestation, the work of Why Not Associates displays a knowledgeable, albeit not always disciplined, command of letterspacing, kerning, and the other basics of typography and design. So, rather than respond in anger, the Why Not designers merely felt sympathy for the book's reviewer. Interesting work often strays from the norm, they say.

This sort of thinking has driven Why Not's talents since they began their studio in 1987, shortly after graduating from London's Royal College of Art. As students, Altmann and his future partners DAVID ELLIS and PATRICK MORRISSEY came under the influence of Dutch designer GERT DUMBAR, who taught there from 1985 to 1987. Dumbar earned international acclaim for the corporate identity he created for Dutch Railways while with the industrial design group Tel Design Associates, The Hague, and he introduced his students to the Dutch concept of combining craft skills with avant-garde ideas. He then challenged them to continually dispute what is conventional and inspired them to fashion their own graphic vernacular. In the case of the future Why Not designers, that dare eventually led them to develop a look that is best described as a mishmash of digitally produced New Wave Constructivism and hallucinatory Internationalism, featuring bright colors, fractured grids, and randomly layered images set against soothing backgrounds of clean, white space.

Next directory, 1989–91.

Some of Why Not's earliest work was done for Next's mail-order catalog, using a combination of Rocco Redondo's photography and illustrations done in Aldus FreeHand.

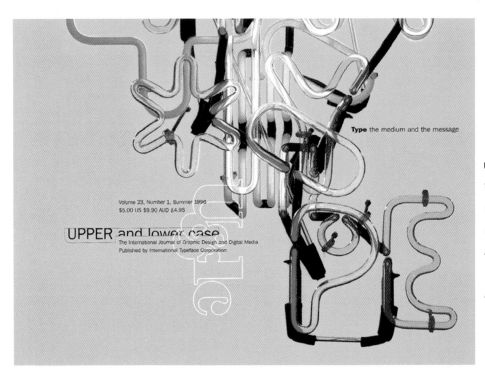

U&lc, *1996.*

U&lc *is both an International Typeface Corporation showcase and a respected design magazine, designed by a succession of guest artists. Editor Margaret Richardson, a fan of Why Not Associates' unconventional, cunning style, asked the firm to design issue 23.*

blue post production
58 old compton street, london W1V 5PA
tel 0171 437 2626 fax 0171 439 2477

Blue Post Production identity, *1995.*

In the late 1980s when the three emerged from design school and decided to open their own studio, they faced a formidable challenge. Most of London's so-called interesting design work was limited to youth-oriented markets such as niche magazines and record companies, and most of this was executed by fearless young designers who had no reason to be timid as they had no staffs or families to support. At the same time, the more establishment studios were doing very conventional work for mainstream clients. True to their name, the designers at Why Not Associates wondered, *"Why not bring interesting work to the mainstream?"* They felt they could inject a sense of intrigue into their projects by relying on the unconventional, no matter what form that might take.

They reasoned that, in a conservative market, a good way to stand out is to be Radical, both in style and in content. Their promotion for the Royal Mail of Britain's Olympic stamp presentation pack, for instance, is unorthodox not so much for its appearance but because it offers a humorous A to Z collection of useless information about the usually reverentially regarded Games. Often, the designers' Radicalism is the result of using an approach similar to that championed by NEVILLE BRODY, who has been a strong influence on European design: a unique typographic voice is created for each project by treating text as both a decorative element and a functional one. Why Not's success to this end prompted Rick Poynor to write in *Typography Now* that their work *"exhibits a typographic abandon . . . and a . . . visual delirium that is formally stunning, but whose relevance to the content is not always clear."*

On the other hand, the designers reason, a market used to Radical design might discover

Royal Mail of Britain Olympic stamp presentation pack, *1996.*

Rosemary Butcher collaborations, 1997. Complete artistic freedom made up for the limited budget of this dance company. Created in Macromind and Aldus FreeHand, the poster is Why Not's take on the precise yet abstract nature of the client's choreography.

Barbican Arts Centre posters, 1998.

These posters reflect their events' themes—a fusion of dance, music, light, and sound by "dumb type" (left) and a collaborative opera/three-dimensional audio-visual performance (below).

a sober execution much more eye-catching. So, scattered in their portfolio of surreal and sometimes illegible work samples are simple, elegant pieces—such as the corporate identity they created for Blue Post Production studios, in which a blue fish swims gracefully away from a splash of blue bubbles in the upper corner of a business card's otherwise unencumbered white background. Only the word "blue" and the company's clearly legible address break up the remainder of the card's space. The same concept is carried through to the other elements of the company's identity system. While elegant in nature, the system exhibits the designers' sense of humor: the blue fish is a type of goldfish, and the company's name "Blue" is set in gold lettering.

Disturbanisms, *1997.*

This poster is for a series of lectures organized by Nigel Coates for the architectural department of the Royal College of Art. Lecture themes included the city, body, horror, and a sense of vulnerability, conveyed via the poster's type treatment and naked human crouched in despair.

This habit of pairing eccentric concept and design technique with subtle humor has led the studio to accumulate a diverse list of prominent clients, from Smirnoff and CBS to fashion retailer Next and Virgin Records. In return for allowing the Why Not designers freedom to practice their curious brand of communication, these clients get memorable work that, in spite of its often bizarre appearance, always speaks directly to its audience and in many cases also appeals somehow to a mainstream consciousness.

craig yoe

Yoe! Studio, Peekskill, New York

dr. seuss on acid

CRAIG YOE has been called *"Dr. Seuss on acid,"* his work, *"bad plumbing."* Garish colors, deranged cartoon characters, mystifying print techniques, and, most of all, a preposterous sense of humorous rebellion prevail. A Yoe piece is also peppered with bizarre icons and slogans that poke fun at life in the corporate domain. One of his studio's promotional brochures, for instance, shows how to moon your boss. On the back of his business card, included among a list of things in which his company specializes is *"butt-kissing."*

Although Yoe proclaims a *"heartfelt desire"* to tell the status quo what to do with itself, he is paid handsomely by Corporate America for

The Art of Mickey Mouse, *1993,* **and The Art of Barbie,** *1995.*
Yoe conceived and art directed this take on how Mickey Mouse is viewed by a hundred top artists, sculptors, and designers worldwide. The book, featuring an introduction by John Updike, turned the Disney licensing attitude "upside down," according to Yoe. The same idea was used for The Art of Barbie. *This time, fashion photographers, models, designers, and others in the field participated. Yoe reveals, "I always wanted to get Claudia Schiffer between the covers, and with this project I succeeded—even if it was just the covers of a book."*

his unconventional ideas, especially those that appeal to kids. PepsiCo, for instance, keeps him on retainer to develop toy premiums for its restaurants' kids' meals (yielding Taco Bell's most successful premium ever—an eyeball straw). Time Warner and Nickelodeon also call him their consultant, as do a host of other megapowers. Even Disney, which zealously guards the sanctity of its characters, not only permitted Yoe to have fun with its most sacred icon—Mickey Mouse—but gladly carries the resulting book, *The Art of Mickey Mouse,* in its own retail outlets.

Yoe is a design school dropout who quit before he was forcibly ejected for staging protest rallies. His professional history nevertheless reads like a who's who of kids' market eminents: art director with Diamond Toy Co.; senior designer with Marvin Glass & Associates, the world's largest toy think-tank (where he helped make plastic vomit and Slime household names); and creative director and vice president/general manager of Jim Henson's Muppets, where Yoe's creative wings really spread. There, he was not only in charge of licensed products but he even designed TV characters and supervised puppet builders. When Jim Henson died unexpectedly in 1990, Yoe had been with him for five years, and

146

Big Boy comic book, *1996.*

Comic books featuring the Big Boy Restaurant mascot have been given to kids visiting the restaurant for decades. For forty years, they were created and produced by Manfred Bernhard (the son of famous poster artist and typographer Lucien Bernhard). Yoe replaced him upon his retirement and has drastically rehauled the book to give it a contemporary edge. His studio does everything from interview celebrities, including Rosie O'Donnell and Melissa Joan Hart (star of television's Sabrina, the Teenage Witch*), and write the copy to draw and color the characters, design the books, and oversee their printing.*

Gross eyeball straw, *1996.*

Yoe is on retainer with several major restaurant chains to conceive and develop premiums for their kids' meals. This eyeball straw for Taco Bell is the restaurant's most popular promotion to date; television ads were withdrawn after only six days when the straws sold out. Yoe says they reflect his studio's motto: "Design that doesn't suck."

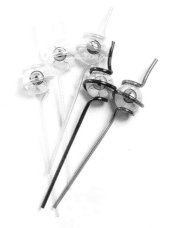

Rock & Barf MuSICKal Instruments, *1997.*

Yoe began producing his own toy line through a division called Yoe! Stuff. Its first offering, which was introduced to the market in 1998, was a weird collection of toy instruments called Rock & Barf and featured the Horror-Monica, the Snot-A-Lotter, and the Slime Whistle. The toys were designed to appeal to "tweens" (kids between the ages of six and twelve) and were distributed by the Ohio Art Company, makers of Etch-A-Sketch.

Yoe! Studio Promotion, *1995.*

Yoe is an accomplished illustrator as well as a designer. Through the years his cartoonlike characters have earned him several Gold awards from the Society of Illustrators.

he decided it was time to strike out on his own. Yoe's aim was, simply, to concentrate on *"stuff"* that he found fun. Success has been quick. He now has a partner, CLIZIA GUSSONI, and twenty-one employees— *"renegades no one else would have,"* he says. His studio today develops everything from set designs, apparel, toys, happy meal premiums, and animation for MTV, Nickelodeon, and the Cartoon Network to toothbrushes and home furnishings. But no matter what the ultimate product, each is injected with the same sensibilities: wackiness, humor, fun, and attitude—lots of attitude.

Yoe's instincts, along with experiences from his childhood and teen years, guide his design solutions. Often, his work has at least some of the look and feel of several unconventional inspirations—he counts *"weird cartoonists named George"* (Carlson, Herriman, and Erling), tattoo artist and sailor Jerry Collins, sign painters of the 1930s era, and *"1950s nude photo model Betty Page"* among them. He considers so-called traditional design sensibilities akin to a pirate's booty. *"All my present and future work is based on the past,"* he says. *"Like a pirate, I either plunder or destroy what I find."*

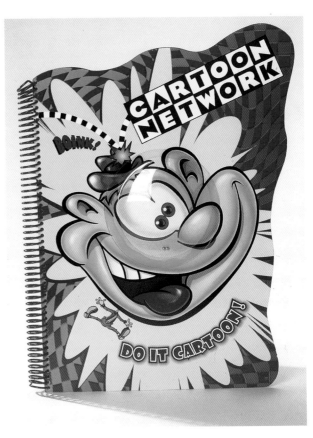

Cartoon Network brochure, *1997.*

This brochure announced the roll-out of the Cartoon Network's licensing program. It was hastily assembled in three weeks, from concept to printing, but the results still earned the studio a 1997 ADDY® award from the American Advertising Federation.

It's obvious that Yoe believes work and fun go hand-in-hand. He is loudly vocal about those designers who criticize their peers for having fun. *"Who are these people?"* he demands. *"Why did they become artists in the first place if it wasn't to have fun and beat the system? Why do people want to do all this boring, stodgy stuff? And why do all the design annuals look the same? It's all this sophisticated stuff with these sophisticated colors and sophisticated type. . . . In art and in life, I want to have fun, break the rules, be wild and crazy. That's why I became an artist."*

progeny

chris ashworth

Substance, Santa Monica, California

swiss grit

When CHRIS ASHWORTH became the art director of *Ray Gun* magazine in 1997, many designers in the United States had no clue as to where or how publisher MARVIN JARRETT had unearthed him. That was not the case in Europe. The native of Leeds, England, had been garnering great attention there for such high-visibility projects as the first MTV Europe Music Awards brochure, a lavish production that he created in conjunction with TOMATO's JOHN WARWICKER and SIMON TAYLOR. The trio also did all the awards' supporting material, from posters and press ads to T-shirts. Ashworth soon attracted more work from MTV and other impressive clients such as WEA Records and the Image Bank. He was already a fast-rising star in European design circles when he landed on America's shore.

Ray Gun, *1997.*

Ashworth had graduated from York College of Arts & Technology in 1990 with a degree in graphic design. Soon after, he and two college friends opened a studio called ORANGE. Most of the work consisted of producing flyers for local nightclubs, of the primitive black-and-white, photocopied ilk usually posted on utility poles and blank walls in night-club neighborhoods. Yet Ashworth's work showed a surprising sophistication. In one poster for Euphona, created shortly after he opened Orange, dynamic blurry images provide a background pattern for the distressed-looking letters that spell out the night-club's name; the name is then repeated in whole in a reverse block of type turned on its side near one corner. The effect is reminiscent of STEFF GEISSBUHLER's famous 1965 brochure cover for Geigy (see page 19). Ashworth's flyers exhibited early facets of what would eventually develop into his current style—one he has christened "Swiss grit"— where Swiss design principles are implicated, but then infused with attitude rather than just an aesthetic style.

In May 1995, Ashworth formed the virtual design studio SUBSTANCE, along with AMANDA SISSONS, who worked with him in their London studio, and NEIL FLETCHER, based in Sheffield. Substance was hired to art direct the music magazine *Blah, Blah, Blah*, a joint venture between Ray Gun Publishing and MTV, which is how Ashworth first met Jarrett. *Blah, Blah, Blah* was sold after six issues, but the two had hit a harmonious chord and Jarrett searched for other projects on which they could collaborate.

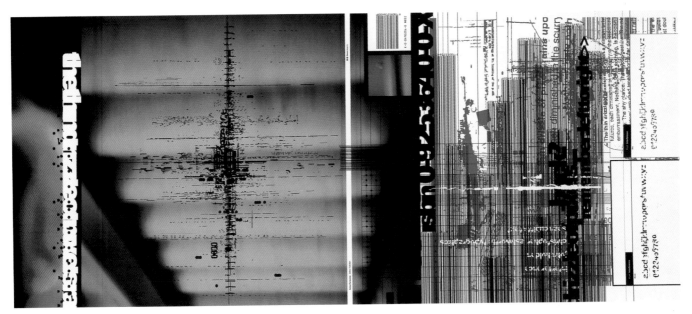

Interference *book jacket, 1993.*

Ashworth developed his "Swiss grit" signature style of design

while working in his off time on Interference, *which*

offers a disturbing visual commentary on surveillance and identity.

The book was written by photography lecturer John Holden.

Blah, Blah, Blah, *1996.*

This music magazine, a joint venture between MTV and Ray Gun

Publishing, was among the first projects to be undertaken by

Ashworth's "virtual studio" Substance, which he established in 1995

with Amanda Sissons and Neil Fletcher. The project lasted

only six months before the magazine was sold, but it eventually led to

Ashworth's job as art director of Ray Gun *magazine.*

Intro   :

2xIntro, *1998.*

The *Ray Gun* retrospective book *Out of Control*, produced in 1996, afforded that opportunity. It also intimately acquainted Ashworth with the magazine, as he had to pore through every issue in his research. That paid off when he got a call to be the magazine's art director, accompanied by Sissons (*"Miss Swiss,"* Ashworth calls her), who aids in its design.

Ashworth had big shoes to fill at *Ray Gun* following DAVID CARSON's exit, who had already secured a spot for the magazine and himself in design annals. (A succession of interim designers filled in during the time it took Jarrett to get Ashworth to the States.) While some might have been overwhelmed at stepping into the post, Ashworth was unperturbed. *"My ideas and surface style were already established before I started on* Ray Gun, *which helped ease any concerns I might have had,"* he told writer JIM DAVIES in the British design publication *Creative Technology* (October 1997).

In fact, Ashworth greatly admires Carson's work, considering him *"the most important designer of his generation,"* and he has sought to refine *Ray Gun*'s look rather than drastically alter it. *"From a Swiss skeleton of design values, concepts and ideas are formed,"* he says. *"Skeleton aside, each issue is void of visual and typographic repetition."* Like Carson, many of Ashworth's ideas for *Ray Gun*'s typography come from the streets. He is especially intrigued by the signs that pepper Los Angeles, which soon peel away to take on a *"gritty"* look in the California sun. And also like Carson, Ashworth takes a true hands-on approach to his design work, manipulating type by hand at various stages of the process to create original art specific to its article. Visual puns, subliminal codes, and typographic messages are generated throughout the magazine, derived from the stories, music, or any other related source. *"The challenge is to push the visual aspect of* Ray Gun *as far and wide as possible,"* Ashworth notes, *"while realizing that we are creating a commercial product."*

The exposure through *Ray Gun* coupled with his conspicuous brand of design have garnered Ashworth many new followers in the United States, including Capitol Records, which hired him to produce the CD cover and promotional materials for a 1998 Robbie Robertson release, and Sprite, which retained him to produce print ads. A photo diary by MICHAEL STIPE of the band REM is also in the works, with Ashworth acting as art director. It would seem, then, that Marvin Jarrett has an almost preternatural ability to predict who will be the next substantial talent in graphic design—as well as the ability to ensure that at least part of his or her fame is secured through work for Ray Gun Publishing. This is being confirmed once again through Ashworth's Swiss grit escapades.

Creative Review, *1996.*

Ashworth created several covers under the Substance banner for Creative Review, *a British design magazine, including this one developed in conjunction with Neil Fletcher. Ashworth's work for* Creative Review *demonstrates much of the same process that he now employs at* Ray Gun, *including his affinity for hand-manipulating type and imagery to create a distressed appearance.*

Robbie Robertson CD, *1998.*

rich roat
andy cruz
allen mercer

Brand Design Co. House Industries, Wilmington, Delaware

a high level of integrity

The work coming from BRAND DESIGN CO. is deceptive. A quick glance might leave one believing that the designers' prevailing mode is sixties and seventies retro. A closer look, however, reveals a not-so-readily defined synthesis of design eras and iconography: go-go girls from the 1960s, customized hot rods à la the 1970s, and type taken straight from old matchbook covers reside alongside bitmapped, stretched-out, digitized fonts. All three partners—ANDY CRUZ, RICH ROAT, and ALLEN MERCER—also have an evident sense of humor and insight into the design eras they pirate in fashioning their look. CHARLES S. ANDERSON is an obvious influence, not for the mid-century vernacular that drives his work as much as for his ability to take found imagery and give it a new identity. The group also borrows from those anonymous commercial artists of the 1960s who specialized in low-budget ads, type, and illustrations.

The company's unusual style was featured in issue 38 of *Emigre* magazine (1996) in an article that demonstrates the designers' keen humor and their ability to poke fun at themselves. It was supposedly authored by BOB SMARTNER, a writer who covers both the design and automotive industries. *"In the face of burgeoning competition, the glamorous greasers at Brand continue to survive by inventing new ideas and tastefully reviving old ones. Instead of trying to follow the other hot rodders out there, they keep their blinders on and cook up new customization techniques,"* he wrote. In reality, Bob Smartner is a product of the Brand designers' vivid imagination, a character inspired by old car ads. Rich Roat is actually the author of the farcical review.

The *Emigre* review may have been fictional, but it is true that the three partners' work is spurred on by something that few, if any, other designers can call their main catalyst—the automotive industry. They embrace the custom paint jobs, pinstriping, lettering, and car advertising of the seventies era when car manufacturers sought to inject their high-powered autos with sex appeal, frequently featuring them

House Gothic, 1997.

House Industries, Brand Design's typography division, released a conservative font called House Gothic. The sans serif typeface, peppered with subtle twists and interlocks, draws its inspiration from the work of Chicago-based commercial artist Alger Zitcus, a well-known print tradesman and typographer who worked from the mid-1920s to the late 1960s. The promotional mailer provides a brief overview of Zitcus's career and traces the roots of his style.

Street Van, *1996.*

Brand Design artist Allen Mercer derived the new fonts in the Street Van typeface

collection from various custom type treatments he had created over several years.

The collection has its roots in the automotive industry, inspired by ads, custom

paint jobs, and 1970s-era advertising.

Bad Neighborhood in a Box, *1995.*

The neighborhood surrounding the group's studio was the inspiration for this

self-promotion.

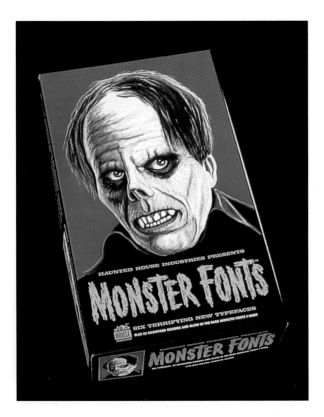

Monster Fonts, 1996.

Hollywood horror movie posters and titles provided the catalyst for this kit by illustrator David Coulson. Andy Cruz created the original Phantom painting based on Lon Chaney's portrayal of the Phantom of the Opera. *House Industries pays royalties to Chaney's estate for the right to use the image.*

draped with scantily clad females or touted by handsome male spokespersons. In a promotion for Custom Papers Group, for instance, the designers hired professional pinstriper ANGELO CRUZ to embellish their poster design with that authentic hot rodder touch. A famous car detailer of the 1960s, ED "BIG DADDY" ROTH, inspired a line of custom free-hand-style typefaces called Rat Fink™ Fonts that the group created and sells through its typehouse subsidiary, House Industries. In fact, custom paint shops and body shapers were part of the target audience, along with advertising agencies and record labels, for House Industries' first sales effort, a card promoting a dozen simple, yet unique faces.

Visitors to any custom auto show can view a plethora of aesthetic overindulges: glittering paint and lavish pinstriping jobs compete for attention with miles of shining chrome bumpers, wheel covers, custom-welded side pipes, and elaborate hood adornments. Brand Design pays tribute to this world via projects that become the print equivalent of a custom car show's decorative extravaganza. Complex printing techniques abound in their work, from debossing and embossing to metallic inks and surprinting, wraparound bands and complicated die-cuts.

Still, they manage to create harmony between such immoderate embellishments and each project's message; the pragmatic is never sacrificed for the dramatic. And, after exerting so much effort to develop a look, they expend an even greater amount to faithfully apply it. *"We call that a high level of integrity,"* **Roat comments,** *"not radical."*

Rat Fink fonts, *1995.*

*Ed "Big Daddy" Roth is famous for custom show
cars he created in the 1960s. The hairy, fly-infested
"Rat Fink" is the central figure in many of his popular
T-shirt designs and is a well-known trademark.*

Pinstripe, *1996.*

*Pinstriping, one of the oldest forms of automotive
customizing, embellishes this promotional poster for
Custom Papers Group.*

scott clum

Rid e Design, Silverton, Oregon

transitions

In his early professional days in the late 1980s, SCOTT CLUM's work was hard to distinguish from that of his design hero, DAVID CARSON. Clum was so adept at mimicking Carson's erratic style that even Carson did a double-take when, while judging a competition, he came across one of Clum's pieces for the first time.

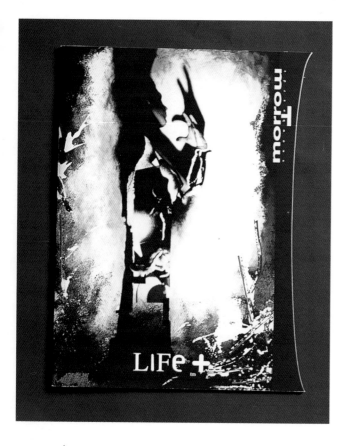

Morrow Snowboards, Life +, 1992.
A gold acrylic painting serves as a compelling image for this catalog cover. Clum often works out ideas through painting and photography.

While Clum retains several Carson qualities in his work today—for instance, his reliance on accidental art, whereby he might incorporate into his design a blob resulting from a bad fax or a dirty photocopier (such as that which adorns his stationery)—he has moved beyond emulating others and is comfortably practicing his own distinctive style. His experimental work with the magazine *blu r* has helped him to this end. *Blu r* began as a way for Clum and photographers TREVOR GRAVES and GAVIN WILSON to show off the overabundance of art that they had produced, but which had gone unsold to clients. In 1992 they resurrected some of these pieces in their own quarterly publication, which is dedicated to bringing together art, music, and comics in an experimental design format. *"Every issue remains a test,"* says Clum several years and many issues later. Wilson still serves as the magazine's music editor, but *blu r* is undoubtedly Clum's child; he acts as design director and offers his studio as production headquarters. The title grew out of Clum's attraction to stop-action photography in which blurred images imply that the subject was moving too fast to photograph. *"In* blu r, *this represents all the hidden levels of art,"* Clum says. The space between the *u* and the *r* in the title is there *"just because it looks good visually,"* just as with the space left between the *d* and *e* in his studio's name.

Since opening Rid e in 1989, Clum has attracted a broad base of clients, including Morrow Snowboards (which he co-owns), Nike, AT&T, Coca-Cola, and Ray Gun Publishing (for which he

Bikini *cover and logo,* 1993.

Huh *logo,* 1995.

Clum wanted "something real" for Huh *magazine's logo, which would also satisfy design director Vaughan Oliver's desire for an "organic" looking image. Rather than attempt to build an image in Adobe Photoshop, Clum created the logo from a photograph of various types of plant leaves.*

Stick, *1996.*

As both codeveloper (with photographer Trevor Graves) and art director of Stick, a Ray Gun Publishing magazine that dealt with the culture of snowboarding, Clum has no problem connecting with readers. In the summer 1996 issue, themed "The New Rock 'n' Roll," Clum makes a humorous plea for subscriptions by using an abstract hand to symbolize begging.

Goddess Snowboards catalog, 1998.

Todd McFarlane's powerful cartoon character Angena plays a starring role in this catalog for Goddess Snowboards, an Oregon-based snowboard manufacturer that caters to women. Clum felt Angena would represent the vigorous attitude of female snowboarders, and he uses her prominently throughout the booklet, supported with action photographs, colorful illustrations of the company's products, and clearly legible blocks of type. A silver imprinted vellum overlay on the cover and the catalog's diminutive size—6 ¾ by 7 inches—lend it femininity.

served as art director of its snowboarding magazine, *Stick*). He employs the same techniques and sensibilities in their projects as he does in *blu r*. Cartoon illustrations abound; swirling, kinetic shapes draw attention to text; and out-of-focus photos of fleeting figures radiate boundless energy and breakneck speed. The work is definitely youth-oriented in appearance and attitude.

Clum also relies heavily on typography to make his work sing. Often, he develops his own faces, and he has a talent for creating ones that go beyond mere lettering to become art objects. They have earned him the attention of NEVILLE BRODY, who asked him to develop a font for his experimental typography magazine, *Fuse*. Specifically, Brody wanted a font that would somehow represent superstition, which was the theme of his thirteenth issue. Clum responded with Burnfont. It addresses the superstition question through how the letters are kerned, with a delicate balance existing between each, just as Clum believes superstition is based on a *"private religion of delicate balances."* He adds, *"I wanted to challenge the communicative value of an image. As in a lot of my work, type plays a dual role—it's image versus graphics and readability."* Burnfont was built entirely outside of the computer, then scanned into it, with the kerning of each letter in the font dependent on the next one to establish a relationship between them. Each letter can also stand alone as a graphic element, which addresses Clum's affinity for dual-functioning type.

Clum's work was also honored in a 1998 retrospective that opened in Portland, Oregon, called *transition*. The show, which attracted eleven hundred people over the course of two weeks, embodied the art, design, and type experiments of his studio from 1990 to 1996, displaying the transitions that occur between fine art—Clum graduated with a fine arts degree from Munson Williams Proctor Institute of Fine Art, Utica, New York, in 1985—and the commercial side of design. *"I have always been captivated by art, its complexities and its ability to move people,"* he notes. As such, the transition show was a fitting summation to date of Clum's work and attitude.

Blu r cover, *1994.*

Guest designer Rick Valicenti created this cover for Clum's experimental arts magazine, blu r *(October 1994). The cover reflects Valicenti's opinion of society and "is really what* blu r *is all about," Clum comments.*

jerôme curchod

Ray Gun Publishing, Santa Monica, California

punked-up

The influence that British design maverick VAUGHAN OLIVER has had on JERÔME CURCHOD is easily noted. Oliver is credited with creating some of the most innovative promotional images in contemporary music, most notably the record sleeves he produced for the progressive London-based label 4AD. He is a master at evoking the moods and textures of the music through an intuitive marriage of type and eclectic imagery. That same aptitude can be seen in Curchod's eccentric style, especially in the designs he produced while art director of the now-defunct *Huh*, working under the direct guidance of Oliver, who served as the music magazine's creative director. Curchod, a Swiss immigrant to the United States, is also heavily influenced by his cultural background. His designs exhibit a clean, almost classic nature that's tinged with the erratic. Mostly, though, his incongruous productions result from an intense desire to fashion new ways to merge text, photography, and illustration. The result is a collision of punk and Swiss sensibilities.

A spread that Curchod developed for a *Huh* article on the band Sponge shows how Oliver's sway and traditional Swiss design standards affect his process. Two neat columns of clearly legible, conservative-looking text fill two-thirds of the right-hand page, neatly linked to the remainder of the spread via a series of interconnecting rules and dotted lines. Only two images are used, yet their cropping and placement make them domineering factors. The first is a large photo of bandmember Vinnie Dombroski that fills a third of the left page. In defiance of the rules of photo cropping taught in publication layout classes, the top of Dombroski's face is chopped off so that the focus rests squarely on his curious gold tooth. The second photo, featuring the entire band, is used almost as an inset with one side running into the right-page gutter (another classic layout taboo) and the other side butting a rule that defines the text grid. The bottom of the photo bleeds off the page. Interlocking rules and the use of various rule styles, along with the jarring photos and their placement, lend the spread its Radical edge. Yet Curchod's selection of neat sans serif type and his allowance for plenty of white space in the background simultaneously inject it with a classic nature.

Huh "Sponge" spread, 1996.

BUSH • THE PHOTOGRAPHY OF MICHAEL STIPE

huh

20

april 96
the presidents
of the united states
of america
interview by
soundgarden's
kim thayil plus a review by
first brother roger clinton

WESLEY WILLIS • 7 YEAR BITCH • HOLE IN IRELAND

Huh *cover, 1996.*

Curchod created the designs, under the guidance of design director Vaughan Oliver,
for Huh, *a Ray Gun Publishing magazine on new music and its musicians.*
In one issue alone the eclectic mixture of articles covered everything from a critique
of rock superstar's hairstyles to a photo essay by Michael Stipe and a review of
William Burroughs's Naked Lunch *audio.*

Huh *"Fashion" issue, 1996.*

Curchod's unorthodox creative style led him to develop this fashion spread using just the
opposite of what one might expect—a maximum amount of text and only one photo.

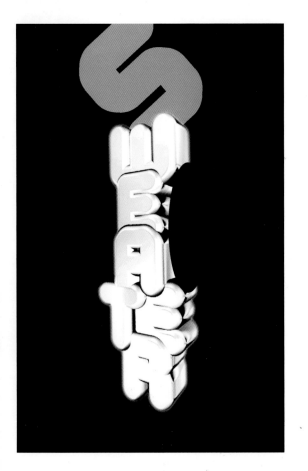

Sweater logo, *1997.*

Curchod's bipartisan creative process is partially the result of being educated in the disparate design cultures of two continents, since he earned his bachelor of fine arts degree studying at the Art Center College of Design's campuses in the United States (Pasadena, California) and in Switzerland. It also is a by-product of self-confidence and keen insight into human nature and current issues. *"I think a lot of people don't understand how to make their designs evolve,"* **Curchod comments.** *"In the realm of 'hip' design, you have to be really sensitive to what's in and what's out, what typeface is just not okay anymore, or what style of photography is outmoded."*

He is continually aiming for such sensitivity in his role as art director of *Sweater* magazine (working with creative directors P. SCOTT MAKELA and LAURIE HAYCOCK-MAKELA), which, like *Huh*, is in the lineup of publications produced by Ray Gun Publishing. Aimed at the dance club scene, *Sweater* also shows Curchod's fascination with what he calls *"altered"* nature. His logo, for instance, demonstrates a keen sense of perspective and organic dimension. While the headlines he created for *Huh* and *Bikini*, another Ray Gun publication, exhibit a playfulness, in *Sweater* Curchod's typographic experiments have become fully developed. Curchod frequently combines headlines and call-outs with icons so that they function more like art objects than words. Blocks of text butt into tightly cropped, emotive photos, or unconventional images bump text aside in a kinetic interplay, à la Oliver and, in a sense, NEVILLE BRODY.

Curchod's attitude about his role in design has also evolved. He now perceives his job as similar to that of a fashion designer who must keep up with public sentiment and find ways to address those attitudes. But while a fashion designer strives to set trends, the consumer is the one who chooses what style best expresses his or her individuality. Curchod urges graphic designers to be equally proactive. They should empower viewers by offering a choice of visual vernaculars, whether Radical or not. Then the viewer can select a vernacular based on individual preference, rather than having to settle for one dictated by some marketing person or an outdated design standard.

Bikini, *1997.*

Though Bikini's *name might sound exploitive, the female images that*
Curchod selected while he served as its art director gave them a sense of power.
His design for the feature on actress Courtney Thorne-Smith, for example,
conveys her strength through striking portraits and a no-nonsense text treatment.

detlef fiedler
daniela haufe
sophie alex

Cyan, Berlin, Germany

preserving cultural contradictions

CYAN has managed to attract an impressive group of high-profile clients since its founding in 1992, most of whom operate within the cultural and government sectors. The downside of this is that their design budgets are often small to nonexistent. This had led to the partners' inside joke: their work *must* be Radical since nobody pays them for it. Innovators have the ideas; followers get the cash.

Nevertheless, Cyan principals DETLEF FIEDLER and DANIELA HAUFE, along with designer SOPHIE ALEX, create quality work for their clients through a balance of superior talent, keen conceptual ability, and the low-cost typesetting and production capabilities of the computer. *"Maybe our work does not submit to conventional ideas of good typography; certainly it is not supposed to actually answer the question of 'good form.' But generally there is an obvious choice between more colorful and costly products, and results which are sound in terms of aesthetics, ecology, and economy,"* Haufe reasons.

The computer has helped the designers do much more than save their clients money. It has proven invaluable in the refinement of their unorthodox look, whereby text, images, and paper are melded into a unified entity using the layering and merging capabilities of various software programs. QuarkXPress, Adobe Photoshop, and Aldus FreeHand, for example, enabled them to create a poster (announcing a series of events at the Bauhaus Dessau) featuring intricate layers of illustrations, photos, and text overlaid upon a dominating female portrait. Muted lime and blue hues offset the dull gray and white of the female image, imparting an organic quality to the poster's otherwise digital appearance.

All three are self-taught in the graphics field, which they decided to take up because they thought it would be fun. Fiedler was originally trained as an architect, Haufe as a typesetter, and Alex as a textile designer, and both Fiedler and Haufe worked at the design studio Grapus before forming Cyan. In spite of their lack of a formal design education and their preference for progressive routes over classic, Cyan's conceptual ideology is tradition-bound. They tend to identify with avant-garde artists of the late 1920s and early 1930s, mostly because of the hardships they endured (especially their low- to

Form + Zweck *nr, 1995.*

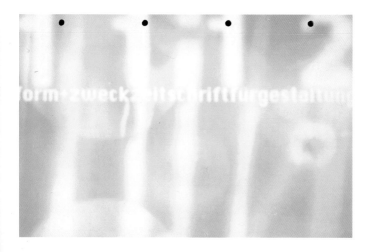

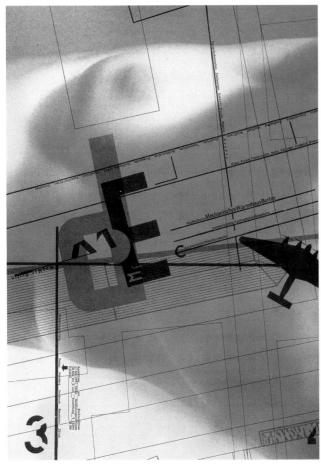

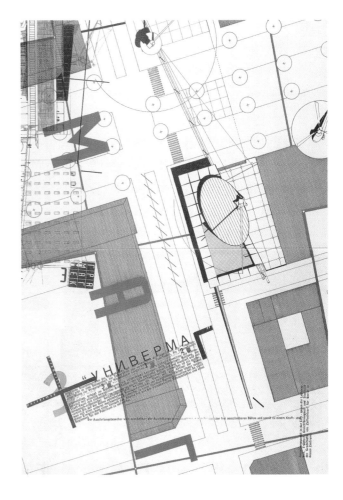

Mag Mec Berlin, *1991.*

Fifteen "warehouse of the future" projects designed by architecture students are showcased in this exhibition catalog (the original projects were on display at Bauhaus Dessau). Cyan created a collage for the cover using material from each project, then humanized the mechanical elements of the architectural process by adding a translucent nude image. Inside, the design of the spreads devoted to each student is intended to reflect the essence of his or her work.

Bauhaus program, *1994.*

The resuscitation of an old railway in Berlin's Dessau area provided the theme for this poster, which announces a bimonthly series of events occurring at the Bauhaus Dessau. The design draws from the Bauhaus Dessau Foundation's identity system, which relies on two-color photo-collages that frequently incorporate female images.

Manifesto of the Communist Party, *1995.*

Cyan wanted to attract young readers to Karl Marx and Friedrich Engels's 150-year-old work (which the designers say still applies today), so they dressed it in a modern outfit of digital techniques and icons, skewed grids, and colors.

no-budgets) and their willingness to allow life and art to overlap—a quality that is a rallying point of many Radical designers. Haufe and Fielder have such a fascination with the fine craft skills of their heroes that they took the time to learn book printing, calligraphy, and how to handset lead and etched-metal type.

At the same time, the Cyan designers are separated from their predecessors by one major fissure: digital technology. At first, their admiration of the past delayed their computer explorations. Eventually, however, the Cyan designers came to realize that in rejecting this technology they were repudiating a fundamental value of the avant-garde movement: its openness to new possibilities. *"The search for a new visual culture that aims to strengthen the individual's independence and thirst for knowledge, experience, and perception is also important,"* Fiedler says.

The computer eventually became a forceful ally in their mission to create designs that do not follow conventional methods, thinking, and techniques, but retain the individual quirks and eccentricities that define a culture. *"It doesn't make sense to reduce ourselves to a money-making machine that participates in large-scale marketing. It doesn't make sense to simplify impulses emanating from culture and society to make them easily digestible,"* Haufe explains. *"Seemingly, this kind of transfer would satisfy the need for originality and exclusivity. However, culture would be deprived of its contradictions."*

Often the content of their work is not easily absorbed, the designers admit, but that is because they refuse to give in to what they view as *"fast-food consumption."* They believe many messages are reduced to sophomoric terms and then conveyed with visual banality just so that viewers may easily *"get it."* However, they believe that reading should be considered an occupation that is directed at gaining experience. If there is difficulty in achieving the experience, it is due to the viewer's particular level of visual sensitivity. *"Form is a question of public interest,"* Haufe says. *"Unfortunately, content is not debated to the same degree."*

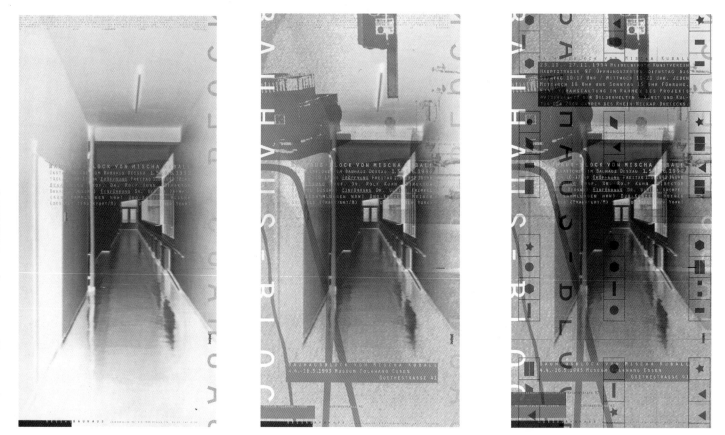

Bauhaus-Block Von Mischa Kuball, *1992–93.*

The exhibition announced in this series of posters occurred in three locations. Cyan linked the different sites by using the same poster design and over-

printing it with a new color (advancing from light to dark), then adding another block of text for each location.

Jeder Hat Jeden Tag Die Möglichkeit, 1991.

Cyan's devotion to social causes is demonstrated in this pro bono poster, which the studio donated to a Berlin campaign

that protested sending German soldiers to the Gulf War.

amy franceschini

Futurefarmers, San Francisco, California

getting under their skin

AMY FRANCESCHINI's work is not conspicuously insurgent. Instead, she employs a Radical subterfuge neatly camouflaged by a painterly palette of soft, muted, earthy tones, an interplay of organic and nonorganic imagery converging on a single plane, and an almost innocent mixture of retro and cartoonish characters. Her print pieces have a naive quality about them, mindful of a faded 1940s Florida postcard one discovers stuck between the pages of an old book. A closer inspection, however, reveals a whole new level of information: layers of translucent messages and images lurk in the background, smirking characters belie innocence, and the tell-tale flaws of digitized type pluck her work out of the past and propel it soundly into the future.

That naïveté is transferred to Franceschini's new media work, too. She has already made a name in interactive design with FUTUREFARMERS (which she operates with partners DAVID HARLAN and STELLA LAI), which was a winner of one of the *Communication Arts* 1998 Interactive Design awards for the studio's own Web site and for its CD-ROM *Stimuli for Wonder.*

Franceschini gives interface design a fresh new look by applying her visual nostalgia to this often overdone and frustrating medium, which is more often than not fraught with huge image files that take way too long to load and scrolling blocks of boring information. The work she did for the online magazine *Atlas* (covering the arts and San Francisco lifestyle) offers insight into her process. Its home page is adorned with a small number of kitschy icons that in some odd way remind one of toy figures from childhood; they are colored in airy pastels and set against a mostly white background. The editorial lineup is announced in headlines or in brief text blocks with links to those subjects' pages via highlighted words or bizarre icons. The effect leaves one in "can't wait" anticipation of the next layer, where, using real-time innovations, one can navigate through interactive essays, an ongoing multimedia novel, photo exhibits, and designers' portfolios, among other things.

Switch hang tags, 1996.

Like most designers, Franceschini begins each project by studying it intensely, striving to discover as much as possible about it and the audience before beginning to design. Yet she differs from the majority of her peers in a major way: when it comes to the final creation, she feels so strongly about presenting the audience with something they

See how easy it is to step-in. Watch the simplicity of the latch as it locks over your bale. Autolock bindings solidly engage both sides of your boot allowing full visibility of the connection. Autolock is never hidden under your boot, never in-between you and your board, never stopping you from stepping in and riding away. See it attach perfectly every time.

Moving the interface out from under your foot puts you closer to your board and closer to the snow.

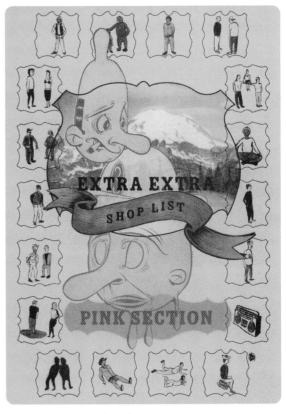

EXTRA EXTRA

SHOP LIST

PINK SECTION

Switch catalog, *1996.*

Franceschini created this catalog for the youthful audience that buys Switch Manufacturing's snowboarding boots. The catalog comes across as a mixture of entertainment and product data, with a look derived from assorted digital and comic book techniques. For instance, much of the copy has a hand-stamped appearance, while many of the background images appear to have been created using a child's toy Spirograph. Quirky characters and art by Barry McGee, Margret Kilgallen, and Chris Johansen reside alongside action photographs of the products in use. Updates to the catalog are produced on inexpensive broadsheet-sized newsprint, with imagery and text retaining the quaint, unique style Franceschini has established for her client.

Switch hang tags, *1996.*

non clog design *"active closure" latch*

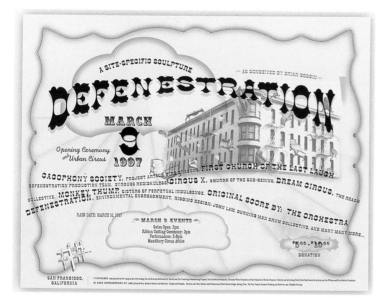

Defenestration, 1997.

The look often associated with Old San Francisco is gently updated in this poster Franceschini created for a site-specific public sculpture event.

have never before seen—something that will make them react—that she doesn't care if they like it or not. Antipathy, she believes, is a better response than none at all.

Franceschini received a BFA from San Francisco State University in 1992, where she majored in photography, then spent another year in design classes at the California College of Arts and Crafts, also in San Francisco. She never finished the program, however, because she felt a void in what it offered and what she sought. *"I had so many ideas in my head, I just needed the tools to produce them,"* she recalls. An internship at *Photo Metro* magazine filled that gap, immersing her in computer technology and forcing her to learn everything quickly and intensely. Aided by the computer, her photography skills and graphic ideas gelled into a cohesive package.

In part, Franceschini is inspired by artist JOSEPH BEUYS, a major influential figure in the post–World War II German and European art scene. Beuys created and produced sculptures, drawings, installations, and performance actions. His desire to explore all art forms even led him to produce concerts, as part of the Fluxus movement in the early 1960s, and his theories on art's social utility influenced a whole generation of creatives. Beuys considered the viewer as important as the art itself, and in his work he strove to create a dialogue between the art object and the beholder. Franceschini viewed a retrospective of Beuys' work in Bonn shortly after his death in 1986 and it left a lasting impression, pushing her to visual solutions that do much more than deliver a single message of "buy me"; they must strike a personal note, too.

Franceschini especially appreciates Beuys for his attempts to make the viewer a participant in his art, just as she now does with her own interactive productions. *"I don't think people want clear design communication,"* Franceschini says of her work. *"This is an era of issues and mixed messages. I think people like to figure things out a little."*

Atlas, *Winter 1997.*

Much of Franceschini's recent work is devoted to Web site development, which allows her great latitude in experimenting with combining print, animation, illustration, and interactive devices. One of her clients is Atlas, *a quarterly online magazine. Shown is the home page she created for the winter 1997 edition.*

MSNBC Web site illustrations, *1997.*

rich godfrey

Fuse, Atlanta, Georgia

you can have it all

RICH GODFREY gracefully travels back and forth between the Radical and the traditional, a journey best exemplified by two drastically diverse projects. First are the bid books he created for the 1996 Summer Olympic Games in Atlanta, while working as senior designer at Copeland Hirthler Design + Communications. The International Olympics Committee (IOC), the entity that determines which city hosts the event, singled out Godfrey's lucidly organized grids as a major reason why Atlanta won this prize over favored Athens, Greece. The IOC now tells other cities that are bidding on the Games to use Atlanta's books as their guide.

At the extreme opposite of the bid books is the work Godfrey does for Divitale Photography under the banner of his new company, Fuse, which he formed with PETE RUNDQUIST in 1992. Ostentatious and expressive, his designs give photographer JIM DIVITALE just what he asked for—attitude. That's because the Divitale pieces are infused with Godfrey's fine arts persona, which is strongly influenced by abstract art. Painter PAUL KLEE's color sensitivity, for example, inspired Godfrey's selection of soft, earthy hues for a Divitale promotional poster otherwise characterized by the layered images and digitized typography typical of a computer production. The palette imparts the poster with an unexpected delicacy. The spontaneity of Surrealist painter JOAN MIRÓ's brush strokes and stream-of-consciousness approach to art are reflected in many of Godfrey's designs, while his digitally layered compositions are mindful of PABLO PICASSO's Cubist experiments.

Atlanta Olympic Committee bid books, 1989–90.

His fine arts sentience explains why Godfrey's work, though often tinged by the Radical—whether it is injected using a startling image, unexpected font selection, or layered compositions—always manages to project an aura of elegance. But also, Godfrey injects his design work with an emotion that fulfills the hunger of his true calling—that of a painter, a dream he set aside while studying at the Ringling School of Art and Design when he realized the financial realities of a career in the fine arts. Instead, he settled on fine arts theory–driven design, a trade-off that has served him well.

Divitale promotions, 1993.

These promotions for Atlanta photographer Jim Divitale simply and progressively put the photographer's unique style to work. The poster in the background, for instance, uses Divitale's photos as a pattern for its "cut-out" letterforms.

Violence and the Crucifixion of Innocence, *1994.*

When Godfrey was asked to design the seventh issue of Pique (a portfolio of cutting-edge artists), he wanted to create an image that would "stop people in their tracks," he says. "I had not previously seen a dead body in a collateral design piece, and thought it would make the strong statement the piece needed."

"I don't agree with a lot of the design that is so in your face you can't enjoy it," **Godfrey says.** *"I think messages get lost in a lot of the way-out type treatments, so I try to keep it a bit lower key and make it a little more sophisticated. If it is just 'cool' looking and doesn't meet the client's objective, then it is not successful. If you can think about the feelings a project should have and what mood it should evoke, plus keep the marketing objective in mind, you can have it all."*

That admonition aside, the best design is like great art, Godfrey believes: it must come from the heart. Keeping that in mind, Godfrey has found both artistic fulfillment and commercial success in producing work that goes far beyond design's mechanics.

The Only Way Out, *1992.*

Godfrey created this sculpture as a form of "self-therapy" by whitewashing an old window frame and then embedding nails in it. Two years later, he put his sculpture to work, using it as the back cover image of Pique *issue 7 (opposite page).*

galie jean-louis

MSNBC, Seattle, Washington

bringing design to life

GALIE JEAN-LOUIS is one of those rare designers who operates within a Radical realm inside the corporate world. A former newspaper designer who used to explore interactive media on her own time, Jean-Louis's work today deals almost exclusively with this new medium. As the executive art director for Seattle-based MSNBC, she relishes the challenge of creating for a medium that is moving more toward a true broadcasting environment, one that allows her to incorporate motion and interactivity into her designs. This latter is an important issue, as Jean-Louis has always striven to bring design to life. *"Film and video have invariably been an impact. Trying to incorporate sound and multimedia, that presence of bringing the page to life, was always my goal,"* she explains.

Primal Screen, 1994.

The influence of Dutch, Russian, and Polish poster designers is seen in this Impulse design.

After graduating from the Ontario College of Art and Design in Toronto, Jean-Louis spent a year in corporate communications doing a lot of television and radio work. But she really came into her own when she returned to her hometown in 1990 to join the *Anchorage Daily News*. Her posterlike front pages for the newspaper's daily entertainment section, Impulse, earned her over three hundred awards—and dramatically increased the paper's sixteen- to thirty-year-old readership. Jean-Louis used elements of illustration, the cinema, and pop culture to give the pages a kinetic quality. Often—armed only with a musician's standard promotional photograph—she had to create a dynamic page under a deadline of only a few hours, or even minutes. Much of her task was accomplished by the creative use of type, like wrapping words and music around the musician's photograph—just as TIBOR KALMAN (one of her inspirations) did in his famous Talking Heads video—and by montaging the images or splashing them with brilliant colors.

In spite of her success, Jean-Louis felt limited by the linear aspects of print work. She missed the many tracks that one encounters in nonlinear design, working with audio, video, and multimedia. She was continually searching for new vehicles for delivering content. *"There's such a tremendous opportunity to rethink the contextural*

Make Room, 1993.

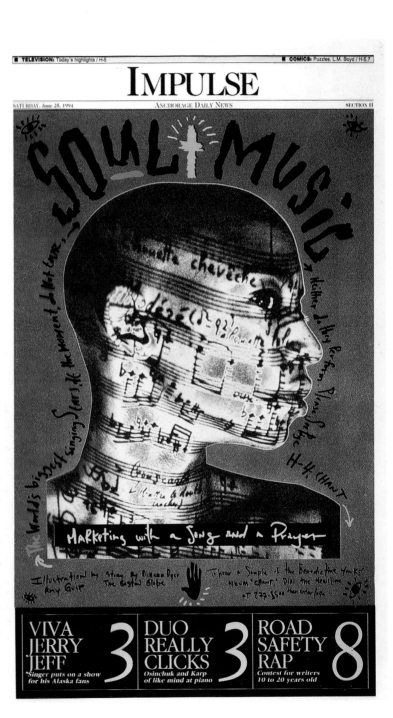

Soul Music, 1994.

Jean-Louis's work for the Anchorage Daily News *was so outstanding that the newspaper ranked third, just behind the* New York Times, *in its number of Society of Publication Designers' awards. Shown is a Tibor Kalman–inspired front page she created for the paper's daily* Impulse *entertainment section, which is aimed at a young audience.*

MSNBC Web page, *1998.*

nature of the product—how people read it, the interactivity of language and illustrative form," **Jean-Louis told** *ID* **magazine (January 1996), after being named one of its top forty international innovators. This trait led her to join MSNBC the following year.**

At MSNBC, Jean-Louis has come full-circle, once again working in motion graphics just as she did before the *Anchorage Daily News.* **This time, however, the medium lets the viewer be an active participant. Jean-Louis's aim is to create interactive news content that allows viewers the opportunity to have real-time experiences.** *"I came here in quest of bringing a new storytelling medium and new storytelling devices to a publication environment. We have opportunities now to tell stories with video, multimedia, audio, with communications vehicles that we didn't have five years ago. The way we sequence the story, the way we have journalists and users interface, is completely new. That was very much of an impetus for me to move in this direction,"* **Jean-Louis says.**

Jean-Louis enjoys interactive work for more than just its design aspects. It also allows her to function as an editor, since she must decide how the information will be delivered to readers, creating fast messages from a model much like that used in advertising. Since most people use the Internet for entertainment, the information must be engaging, too. The MSNBC Web site, for instance, features a look and structure that has shifted from the typical vertical, scrolling screen of most sites to an enhanced, easy-to-use horizontal billboard style of presentation. Information is displayed in easily legible typefaces, with a cascading menu system that enhances navigation by providing a quick, comprehensive look at the day's news. Bright colors, catchy illustrations and photographs, automated slide shows, and audio clips round out the site's visual components.

With no established rules to follow, Web site design also affords her the opportunity to pioneer new frontiers. *"I have always been attracted to a maverick design outpost,"* **she says.** *"I want to create hybrid design solutions that bring together opposites."* **As the Web becomes more layered and multifaceted, Jean-Louis's desire is to move toward a design genre of minimalism for the user—one that traverses a cultural, global, and iconic reference for a new audience.** *"There is a spiritual and mythological component that is a conduit in all aspects of my problem solving, regardless if it is new media, film, print, or the Web,"* **she explains.** *"Whatever you produce should ask more questions than what the problem solves and push you forward to new design landscapes."*

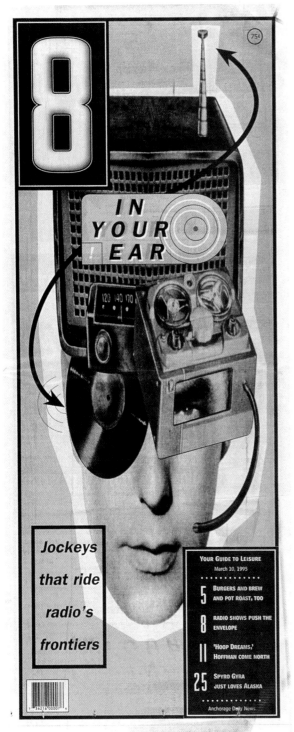

MSNBC Web page, *1998.*

This Entertainment section feature on "The Revival of Vinyl" is among Jean-Louis's favorites for its bold colors and catchy use of typography. She art directed the piece, which was designed by Sofia Vecchio.

8, *1994–95.*

"8" is the Anchorage Daily News's *weekend arts and entertainment section. When the paper needed to lower its budget because of rising newsprint prices in 1994, Jean-Louis developed this cost-cutting, eye-catching design. She vertically bisected the section's normal broadsheet size to give it a new slim format; inside pages use elongated letterforms created by type designers Denis Ortiz Lopez and Mike Bain.*

geoff kaplan

General Working Group, Los Angeles, California

the visual alchemist

GEOFF KAPLAN has worked with some of the best modern studios in the United States, including Los Angeles–based SUSSMAN/PREJZA DESIGN & CO., INC., and APRIL GREIMAN, INC. But he decided to leave such lofty posts because he was never quite satisfied with his work. Kaplan felt a strong urge to probe design's cultural, political, and personal significance, and after seven years of professional experience, he decided going back to school was the best way to further his exploration. After all, one of his mentors, April Greiman herself, had advised him to *"trust his instincts."* His first design degree was from Carnegie Mellon University (in 1987), but this time he chose Cranbrook Academy of Art because of the school's focus on exploring how language informs and creates a condition of multiple meanings. He graduated in 1997, forever changed by the experience.

A graduate studies catalog he created for the school in 1996 shows how Cranbrook affected Kaplan's way of thinking and working. While at Sussman/Prejza, he was a master at applying the company's rational design approach, most notably seen in the studio's celebrated identity program for Southern California Gas Co., a project on which Kaplan served as senior designer. The identity project employs a graphically strong, modernistic-looking white flame logo set inside a vertical blue rectangle. The logo synthesizes the company's nature in a manner that is straight to the point, effortlessly identifying both it and the market in which it operates.

Kaplan's sixteen-page, two-color Cranbrook booklet, however, is a clear departure from this approach. It is much more visually complex, and it attempts to communicate contextually on several levels. His experiment begins with the cover, which features a miniature folding chair bumping into the Cranbrook headline, set against a background of what appears to be brickwork. *"The chair,"* **Kaplan says,** *"is used as a*

A World in Tune, 1994.

Designer April Greiman's influence is seen in this poster Kaplan created shortly after opening his own studio. It represents his break from the "super-rational modernist approach" he had previously used in his work.

American Center for Design, Living Surfaces, *1998.*

The theme for the sixth annual Living Surfaces Conference (held each year in Chicago) dealt with how new media affects traditional narrative paradigms.

Kaplan reflects the questions raised by the conference by focusing on one of the world's oldest books, the Bible, and how it incorporates many of the so-called

revolutionary communication ideas brought on by the new media, such as multiple authorship under one cover. "It also has no beginning or end," Kaplan

notes. "You can open it up to any section and start reading." Kaplan worked on the project with his former Cranbrook teacher, Katherine McCoy.

Intersections and Interstices, *1996.*

This brochure documents a collaboration between students in Cranbrook's ceramics, fiber, and metalsmithing departments, as well as that of Kaplan and fellow design student Mikon van Gastel. Kaplan and van Gastel used overexposed photographs, fractured leading, randomly placed color surprints, and reversed type that intentionally disappears into the imagery to represent the breakdown of barriers that might exist between various art media.

Cranbrook Academy of Art catalog, 1996.

metaphor for unfulfilled meanings and represents the school's evolution from the Arts and Crafts movement and its emphasis on well-designed objects." The chair and brickwork are overlaid with a translucent pattern that elicits a sense of being underwater. An enigmatic image that appears to be a set of large black "wings," imparting a message of freedom and soaring, vertically dissects the cover in the left quadrant. The wings icon also separates the chair imagery from an obscure, blurred green, black, and cream pattern that bleeds off the left side of the page and around to the back cover, where it comes into clear focus and its true nature is revealed—a tree.

Inside, the catalog contains a narrative on the school's history of risk-taking, as well as general academic information, relayed in a simple visual manner—text is set in clearly legible type, illustrations are small photos colored in either black and white or green, and layouts employ two-column grids with ample white space for a clean, concise look. Yet, the viewer also finds a surprise: the catalog cover is actually a clever folder designed to hold yet another booklet (Kaplan calls it a *"sub-brochure"*) describing each of the school's departments. The booklet also visually conveys the Cranbrook commitment to risk-taking that is described in the main catalog's text. Filled with obscure images and abstract type, this sub-brochure is held in place in the folder via a complex die-cut tab that mimics the wing shape found on the cover. Thus, Kaplan demonstrates a pragmatic side by separating the school's consistent information from that which is likely to change, allowing Cranbrook to easily update the catalog at a minimal production cost. Yet, his Radical nature comes through in its progressive visual countenance.

Part of Kaplan's keen appetite for discovery comes from his belief that design is beginning to realize its poignancy and its potential to help shape society. This is especially true of motion graphics, with which he has been intrigued since childhood. As a consequence, he is moving further into time-based media and exploring how graphic design laps into film. A project titled "Do I See? Do I K(no)w?" offers an example. Kaplan and AKIRA RABELAIS, a specialist in abstract digital synthesis and software design, collaborated to examine how various data, such as text and image, can be interpreted into sound and what happens when that same sound is turned back into an image. The experiment began with Rabelais writing a software program that translates digital information from

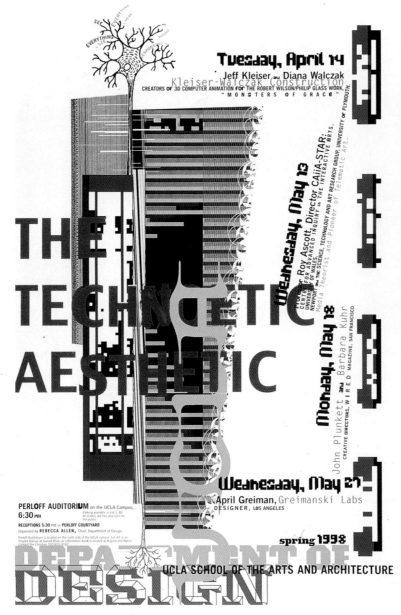

Tuesday, April 14
Jeff Kleiser and Diana Walczak
Kleiser-Walczak Construction
CREATORS OF 3D COMPUTER ANIMATION FOR THE ROBERT WILSON/PHILIP GLASS WORK,
"MONSTERS OF GRACE"

Wednesday, May 13
Professor Roy Ascott, Director CAiiA-STAR:
CENTRE FOR ADVANCED INQUIRY IN THE INTERACTIVE ARTS,
UNIVERSITY OF WALES, NEWPORT
THE SCIENCE, TECHNOLOGY AND ART RESEARCH GROUP, UNIVERSITY OF PLYMOUTH.
Media Theorist and Pioneer of Telematic Arts.

Monday, May 18
John Plunkett and Barbara Kuhr
CREATIVE DIRECTORS, WIRED MAGAZINE, SAN FRANCISCO

Wednesday, May 27
April Greiman, Greimanski Labs
DESIGNER, LOS ANGELES

spring 1998

THE TECHNOETIC AESTHETIC

PERLOFF AUDITORIUM on the UCLA Campus,
6:30 PM
Parking available in Lot J, $5
All Events are free and open to the public

RECEPTIONS 5:30 PM in PERLOFF COURTYARD
Organized by REBECCA ALLEN, Chair, Department of Design
Perloff Auditorium is located on the north side of the UCLA campus. Lot #3 is on Hilgard Avenue at Sunset Blvd; an information kiosk is located at Hilgard and Wyton.
Contact Tim Christian (310) 825-9287.

DEPARTMENT OF DESIGN

UCLA SCHOOL OF THE ARTS AND ARCHITECTURE

The Technoetic Aesthetic, 1998.

Kaplan and Gail Swanlund, with whom he frequently collaborates, created this announcement for the UCLA Design and Media Arts Department's lecture series. It was selected for inclusion in the American Center for Design's 100 Show.

sound and text into imagery. Kaplan used it to digitally compile a movie from television footage, an early Surrealist film, a speech synthesis of the introduction to *The Book of Five Rings*, and his own typographic creations. He then made three more movies by building on the components of each subsequent one as the basis for the next and compared the results.

The process is complicated, but Kaplan believes that such studies will help him understand both the film process itself and its social-political implications. Besides, he says, *"Those who master time-based design now will define and direct the professional design landscape of the future."*

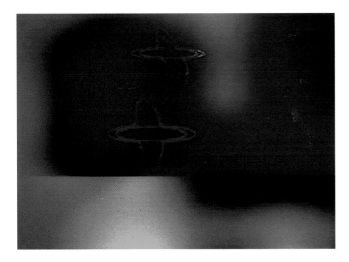

Do I See? Do I K(no)w?, 1997.

gigi biederman
david karam

Post Tool Design, San Francisco, California

coming to terms

The owner of POST TOOL, the hardware store, was slightly irritated when he discovered that his upstairs tenants had taken his store's name for that of their design studio. At the time of the appropriation, GIGI BIEDERMAN and DAVID KARAM never anticipated the kind of following their offbeat designs would soon attract. They also never dreamed so many people would call the hardware store looking for them. Luckily, the store owner good-naturedly directs potential clients to the proper place, although he occasionally grumbles that all he gets for his efforts are the proceeds from a few screwdriver sales.

Clients, from Warner Records and Steelcase Seating to Sprint Telecommunications, seek out Post Tool (the design firm) for its fluid, three-dimensional execution, rich colors, humor, and especially, its entertaining storylines. Most of this work is produced on computer, which Karam and Biederman consider another art medium. And since the computer is still new enough that no formal digital design rules have yet been established, they feel it offers boundless artistic freedom. On a more practical side, it also allows them to quickly produce complicated compositing and, in the process, suggests endless variations on their own preconceived design schemes.

Their print work is a reflection of their interactive style, with the static images often made to appear as if they were freeze-framed from an animation, using swirls of white shadows to suggest motion. Their layered color palettes evoke an aura of translucency like that seen on the Web. Type doesn't just sit on the page in a Post Tool creation; it often is injected with a fluid sense of movement through the designers' selection of full, rounded lettering and use of diminishing sizes to lend perspective.

While Post Tool's print work is intriguing, it is in inter-active media that the designers truly come into their own. Their studio's Web site (www.posttool.com) shows how they effectively cross barriers

Jamming the Media, 1997.

Karam created the cover for this book on how to pirate media. He used frequency as a common element to represent electronic media.

Cardinal Directions, *1997.*

This piece, created for a gallery, represents Post Tool's exploration of the computer's role in art. How the artwork's characters are navigated through the information echoes the issues often encountered in content development.

Multimedia Graphics, *1995.*

The abstract cover of this multimedia design survey provides an umbrella for a large range of graphic styles, while its horizontal orientation makes a reference to laptop computers.

Post TV Web site, 1997.

between education and popular culture, past and present, and between art and design using technology's vast capabilities. The Web site is set up like a fictional television station called Post TV. The home page is a simple production, with a spinning three-dimensional TV icon (which looks suspiciously like a cross paired with a victory sign) centered in a white swirl against a background of vertical pastel bars that mimic the horizontal color bars of a real television. The viewer can select from a menu of six "programs" by clicking on a program's corresponding icon (once again, a simple rectangular TV-screen shape with the name of the program centered inside) spanning the bottom of the page.

Once into the program pages, viewers move far beyond simplicity into an entertaining odyssey of serious content, humorous parody, and technological sophistication. The designers also take advantage of the computer's shortcomings, rather than try to overcome them. In the Post Tool news cast, for instance, they developed a Supermarionette-like anchor named Tom Bland (mindful of Colonel Steve Zodiak from Gerry and Sylvia Anderson's 1961 television puppet show, *Fireball XL5*), who delivers a tongue-in-cheek commentary on current events, moving in jerky motions that parody the motion graphics of the Internet before real-time animation. His delivery is accomplished in broken audio, aping the shaky motions of the newscaster. The "over the shoulder" graphic icon that typically accompanies newscasters is one often associated with the news—a globe spinning on its axis. This one, however, lurches.

In "JunglEmail," a three-dimensional, brightly colored cartoon character (also named Bland) drives through a fanciful, animated landscape in his rocketship car while listening to his E-mail messages. The cartoon ends with him receiving a cellular-phone sex call from his girlfriend that causes him to get excited and crash. Or, click on one of the tin cans at the bottom of the page and visit another Post TV character, such as Joey Valley, a lounge lizard who sings "King of the Web" (to the tune of Roger Miller's "King of the Road"), or Alien Rapper. Learn if you're a loser by taking Tom Bland's alcoholics test, or watch for hours as a three-dimensional cartoon

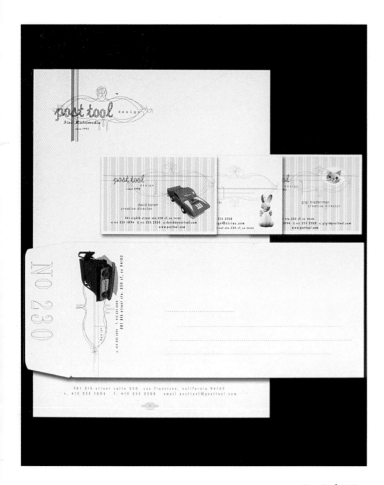

Post Tool stationery, 1997.

caterpillar shouts for its master and tries to cross a fish-filled stream—over and over again.

Diametrically opposite to the site's humor are such features as *Homing In*, TODD HIDO's "photographic prose" that is an elegant combination of moving words and ghostly photographic images accompanied by tranquil music. Then there is *Bedtime Stories*, perhaps the most poignant statement about technology to be found on the Internet. It features an author's voiceover reading a story, visually accompanied by nothing—there is just a blank screen.

Karam and Biederman met while taking design courses at California College of Arts and Crafts (CCAC), San Francisco, then they formed Post Tool in 1993. Before attending CCAC, Karam studied music and computers at the University of Texas, while Biederman earned degrees in fine arts and art history from Skidmore College, New York, and in environmental design from Parsons School of Design in Paris. They felt that they would make a good team because their backgrounds could help them merge what they consider two extremes: fine art and technology.

In their design process, the computer is the formal element that allows them to produce multimedia works of social commentary. *"Interactive media attempts to recreate the free flow of associations of the unconscious mind. Image, text, and sound is the vocabulary of multimedia. The computer is the glue that ties ideology and imagery together,"* Karam comments. Through this menagerie of elements, Post Tool has created a vocabulary spanning print, interactive design, video, animation, and installation.

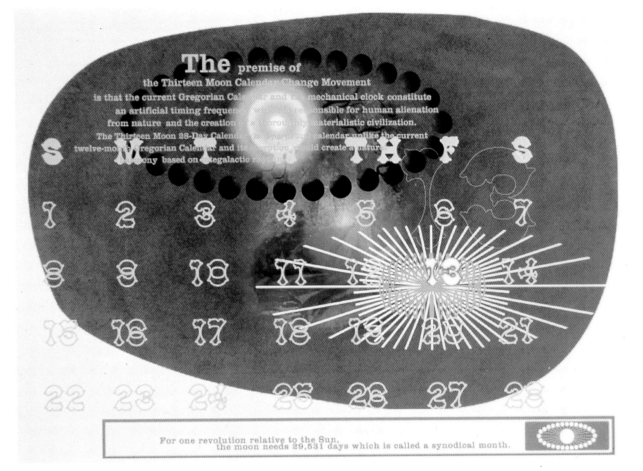

The premise of the Thirteen Moon Calendar Change Movement is that the current Gregorian Calendar and the mechanical clock constitute an artificial timing frequency responsible for human alienation from nature and the creation of a grossly materialistic civilization. The Thirteen Moon 28-Day Calendar is a calendar unlike the current twelve-month Gregorian Calendar and its adoption would create a natural harmony based on intergalactic rhythms.

S M T W T F S

1 2 3 4 5 6 7
8 9 10 11 12 13 14
15 16 17 18 19 20 21
22 23 24 25 26 27 28

For one revolution relative to the Sun, the moon needs 29,531 days which is called a synodical month.

13 Months Calendar, *1996.*

The thirteen-month calendar preceded the Gregorian calendar, the one almost universally used today and which evolved from the Roman calendar reformed in 46 B.C. by Julius Caesar. Many believe it is much more accurate than the Gregorian calendar and more in harmony with the universe. To reflect the calendar's natural implications, Post Tool developed an organic-looking design solution in which all imagery was created by hand.

stefan sagmeister

Sagmeister, Inc., New York, New York

schizophrenia

STEFAN SAGMEISTER's early design work of the mid-1980s could be described as very functional and cold. His audiences found it aloof and inaccessible, so he began to alter his style, hoping to relate better. Along the way, Sagmeister found that he was venturing *"an itsy-bitsy bit"* into Radical territory—and he liked it. Periodically, he explains, boredom sets in, leaving him with the urge to *"go crazy"* and develop something that jolts viewers.

Sagmeister's formal side is a product of his education at the University for Applied Arts in Vienna, Austria, followed by further studies at the Pratt Institute in New York, from which he graduated in 1988. His wilder facet comes from his playful, slightly subversive personality, which was amplified by a stint working with TIBOR KALMAN at M&Co. Labs, Inc. He also freelanced in both New York and his native Austria, as well as worked with the Hong Kong office of LEO BURNETT, before returning to the United States to open SAGMEISTER, INC., in 1993. The body of Sagmeister's work reveals a design schizophrenia: one moment he's creating traditional designs that would make even MASSIMO VIGNELLI nod in assent, and the next he's torturously pushing, shoving, stretching, and compressing text and then pairing it with outrageous images that make the viewer laugh, cringe, or at the least, do a double take.

Sagmeister developed his current reputation while working in Hong Kong in the early nineties. He was quietly going about his business when he was asked to design the Southeast Asia Association of Accredited Advertising Agencies (4A's) 1992 call-for-entries poster. The solution to him was obvious, but bold. Many designers would never have had the nerve to create a poster for a group of executives that featured a lineup of people baring their bottoms, especially not in the conservative Far East. The notoriety he received from the 4A's poster—which included coverage on the front page of the *South China Morning Post*, Hong Kong's largest daily newspaper—still follows wherever he goes. The poster has become his trademark.

Just as with his former boss, Kalman, Sagmeister's design concepts often exhibit a sense of irony and, sometimes, even poke a little fun at his clients. Yet he does it all with such skill, good humor, and in such a low-key manner that he gets away with it nearly every time.

Pro-Pain, 1994.

Part of being a great designer, Radical or traditional, is knowing when not to design. Sagmeister shows wisdom to that end with this cover he created for a hard-core band's CD. The haunting image needs no embellishment.

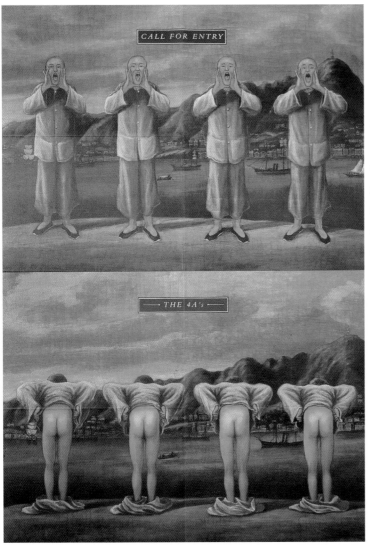

The 4A's, *1992.*

This invitation for an advertising and design awards show in Hong Kong created a scandal in the conservative Far East. The poster was painted by copy painters in a Hong Kong factory who normally reproduce Old Masters' works for hotels and boardrooms. Since the painters can only copy existing works, Sagmeister had to provide composite photographs of what he wanted— which is how his own backside wound up on the poster.

YMO, *1993.*

This CD cover for Ryuichi Sakamoto and YMO (Yellow Magic Orchestra) includes ten different covers; the consumer then chooses his or her favorite. Each cover contains a coded message by American artist Jenny Holzer that can be read only when the CD is in its plastic jewel case.

Sonny Sharrock CD, 1996.

Sonny Sharrock died before the release of this last recording, Into Another Light. *Sagmeister's design simply and poignantly pays tribute.*

While Sagmeister enjoys proffering up an occasional visual disturbance, he's learned there are limits. His most disquieting design project was undoubtedly a CD cover for a hard-core band called Pro-Pain. The cover featured an unretouched photo of a woman's body undergoing an autopsy (her entire chest was split open), taken from police archives. The design received an equal amount of criticism and praise, yet it is the latter that leaves Sagmeister questioning whether he should have used the photo. *"The praise worried me the most,"* **he notes,** *"people saying such things as 'that cover with the cut-up chick is really kicking ass.' I thought long and hard before releasing the cover, but if I were to make the decision again today, I would do it differently."*

From experience, then, Sagmeister urges designers to consider the consequences of their work before going purely for shock value. Check out the project from all stances, from client to product to the consumer. If the visual solution needs a traditional form and style, then that is the path which should be taken. Still, Sagmeister says, occasionally it doesn't hurt to attack the problem from a Radical point of view and *"get something out with some grit to it."*

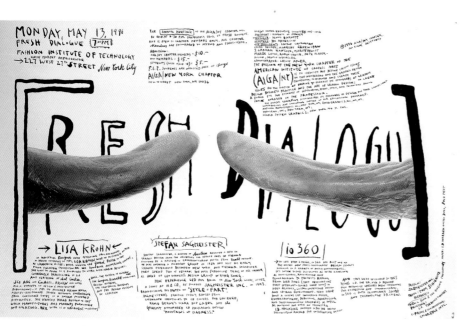

Fresh Dialogue, 1996.

Sagmeister created this poster for the AIGA (New York chapter) to announce its Fresh Dialogue *lecture. As with the 4A's poster, he relied on the obvious— and got scandalous results. He explains, "Tom Schierlitz shot two cow tongues with a 4-by-5 camera. Somehow they came out phallic. We didn't mind. Some AIGA members did."*

Lou Reed poster, 1996.

This poster was inspired by a New York art exhibition at a SoHo gallery featuring the work of Shirin Neshat, a Middle Eastern artist who wrote on the hands and feet of her subjects in Arabic. When Sagmeister read the lyrics for "Trade In", a very personal song in which Reed admitted his need to change, it reminded Sagmeister of how personal Neshat's work was, so he wrote the lyrics for "Trade In" across Reed's face to evoke that same sense of intimacy.

lee schulz

California Institute of the Arts, Valencia, California

the reactionary

LEE SCHULZ is at the beginning of his design career; at the time of this writing, he was a student in the CalArts MFA program, having earned a BFA in visual communication design at the University of Dayton, Ohio. Yet he has already attracted the kind of attention from his teachers and associates that promises much to come. He considers his work more reactionary in its formal construction than intentionally Radical, and though his design process is obviously in a state of transition and development, he exhibits one constant vital to success: he always evaluates and then reevaluates the message, looking at not only the imagery but the context in which it will appear. *"Visually aggressive work is not necessarily good work, nor is it necessarily effective,"* he reasons. *"However, when treated properly and developed according to its intended receivers, it can have tremendous impact. Certainly, those are my aims."*

How a project's pragmatic concerns will work with the audience's social and aesthetic biases and historical interests are important pieces that help him solve each visual puzzle. His consideration of these elements can be seen in his student project *Phone Management*, completed in late 1995. The goal was to produce a study of an object with history, significance, and purpose in society. Schulz chose the telephone as his subject, then pursued the idea of degraded type, spurred by the coarse scribblings often found in pay-phone booths, combined with the ideas of information transfer, chaotic information, and the phone viewed as not just a communications instrument but as an entity in itself. He produced a series of four posters that feature layers of graffiti type over close-up images of telephone parts (dial pads, ear sets, and so on) overlaid upon ghostly shadows of familiar phone booth components. An old Ma Bell logo promotes the idea of the phone's history, while the text spells out its significance to society.

At this early stage in his development, Schulz is heavily influenced by many sources: film, music, books, GUSTAV KLIMT, Baroque architecture, JEAN-MICHEL BASQUIAT, and JIMI HENDRIX among them. Painting, however, is his main impetus, impressing on him the power of surface tactility, transparency,

Art Center Dayton, 1995.

Schulz created this design show's call for entries, striving to clearly articulate the visual complexity and nature of this particular show's topic, "everything but the kitchen sink." He saw it as a pun on plumbing and on the call for entries.

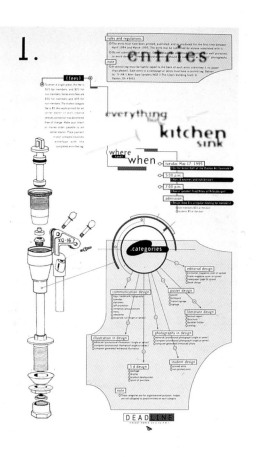

Ohio Stories *poster,* *1995.*

The two filmmakers who produced Ohio Stories *stuck to their roots by creating this film in and about their native state. Schulz played up his clients' backgrounds and the film's storyline in this promotional poster by emphasizing Midwestern culture and its idiosyncrasies. Layers of text make up the industrial cityscape seen in the poster's background.*

light, value, textures, and patterns. Its influence can be seen especially in how he positions type and imagery to interact on both the surface of the project as well as within its space, such as in the *Phone Management* posters.

Beyond that, he looks to his peers to keep him grounded, exhibiting a maturity not often seen in someone just starting out. It is important to know what others are doing, he believes, along with their passions and interests, and to constantly question them regarding their values and concerns. *"Otherwise, it is very easy to lose perspective,"* **Schulz says,** *"and in this field that can be both dangerous and devastating."*

Peter Feldstein announcement, *1995.*

Schulz adapted Peter Feldstein's visual language to his own typographic execution in this announcement of the visiting artist's lecture.

Phone Management, *1995.*

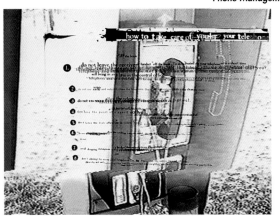

Basquiat, 1995.

Schulz created this poster's image as a contradiction to a noted excerpt from a Jean-Michel Basquiat notebook for a show at the Art Institute of Chicago. The poster is reminiscent of P. Scott Makela's work, but exhibits a more restrained typographic control.

Lunar Chronicles CDs, 1995.

His client had already developed the Lunar Chronicles' theme and planned to release the three CDs, featuring local Ohio bands, on the full moons of May, June, and July. The record label wanted that idea expanded visually for the CD packaging, so Schulz concentrated on moon landings, astronauts, and the obsession with these subjects as heroic and mythological science-fiction entities as well as objects of sci-fi kitsch.

stan stanski
phil yarnall

Smay Vision, New York, New York

bizarre antics

A spirited, occasionally twisted sense of humor is a defining factor in the efforts of many young Radicals. That is especially true of the work and personalities of SMAY VISION **partners** STAN STANSKI **and** PHIL YARNALL. Humor has always been a major contributor to their designs, often injected merely "for kicks." It is exhibited in layouts that mimic the profile of an ample human rump, in their chunky black typefaces with names like "Duh," and through a nightmarish creature adorning their promotion cards that could be the evil twin of Bibo, the signature character from Archie McPhee (a popular Seattle oddities store). A sense of humor is so crucial that the Smay Visionists consider the most stinging remark ever made about their work to be "It's not funny." The critic was referring to their Mating Squirrels Christmas card; they responded by taking her off their mailing roster.

The list of Smay inspirations offers insight into the designers' collectively contorted persona. In their downtime, which was frequent in the early days of their studio (founded in 1993), they would steal images from old "girly" magazines and use them in self-promotion cards. *"We still do this,"* **Stanksi admits,** *"but now we use some of the more obscure images in our clients' projects, too."* Drunken doodlings and the crude art that often adorns cocktail napkins inspired the pair to create such offerings as Drinkiepoo type and the cocktail-laden card (complete with drink recipes) that promotes it, while an old rusty tire sign inspired the rustic, fading letters of Rhino Flex type. *"Cheesy religious artifacts"* of all denominations, found in several of their self-promotion cards, are further peculiar instigators for their raucous eclecticism.

Ditch Croaker, Secrets of the Mule, *1996.*

While their work displays no obvious knowledge of design history, the two are steeped in its traditions. Both graduated from the Tyler School of Art in Philadelphia in 1990. They also studied in Rome for a year during this time, so their education alone probably qualifies them to work at any studio they choose. They opted, however, to strike out on their own so they could produce *"fun"* work that relates to its market in a way that the legendary PAUL RAND, a vehement Radical critic, would certainly have approved of, but whose look he would never have condoned.

Drinkiepoo font and poster, 1995.

Oscar Wilde, 1995.

The Guitarists Formerly Known as Chicks, 1995.

They come from all walks of life, express themselves in countless ways, and command respect among their peers. They are getting as much attention as their male counterparts and are a force to be reckoned with—and acknowledged. This is not some feminist wet dream but is, in fact, the current state of women guitarists. For the first time since guitars got plugged into amplifiers, women are equals to their axe-wielding male counterparts. Women guitarists are no longer content to be ghettoized into "acceptable" musical categories such as folk and country, and now can be heard playing everything from heavy metal to jazz, and especially alternative rock. They are a fresh voice on the pop music scene, and are inventing new modes of expression for the guitar that could only be the result of their unique perspective. For one thing, today's women guitarists had little in the way of female role models, so their outlook on the guitar has been influenced by both sexes, something that just can't be said for most male guitarists. Women were never allowed to play by the rules, so they are often better at breaking them.

(The Guitarists formerly known as Chicks)
by Lee Sherman

Beautiful People self-promotion, 1996.

Their wit and banter might shake the stodgy entities who make up most of Corporate America like a hula dancer on speed, but the studio's clients are for the most part equally bizarre and appreciate their antics. Many are record labels, rock trade publications, and musical groups with names like the Meat Puppets and Ditch Croaker. They find the pair's work refreshing and right on target for their young audiences, caring little at all if the theories of marketing are applied to their projects.

The Dwellers, **Whatever Makes You Happy** *CD package, 1995.*

A package for Ditch Croaker's 1996 *Secrets of the Mule* CD exemplifies Stanski and Yarnall's intuitive ability to hone in on what an audience will relate to. The designers mixed primitive pinhole photographs of an assortment of odd images (including plastic pigs, cacti, and pickup trucks) with an equally bizarre illustrated landscape. Chunky type set in a crudely drawn sunburst and a palette of eerie blues and browns complete the package's strange appearance. The setting seems to have little, if anything, to do with the CD's title, yet it definitely conveys the band's alternative proclivity. And it definitely grew out of the designers' clairvoyant design process and the nature of the group's music rather than from any marketing considerations. *"Market research, shmarket research,"* **Stanski says.** *"Safe, researched design is for wimps. If something looks groovy, people generally dig it."*

gail swanlund

Swank Design, Hollywood, California

the eccentric blip

Writer VICKI MONGAN **once called designer** GAIL SWANLUND *"an eccentric blip in the evolutionary path of a culture that sends it in a new direction."* **A descendent of Minnesota's original, steadfast Swedish settlers, Swanlund does defy the norm of what most consider the dependable, down-to-earth Midwesterner. She blames it all on California.**

Shakespeare, 1994.

Swanlund wanted this poster to barely hold together formally, yet possess a certain sweetness—thus, her playful, flowing typography intermingles with lighthearted, sometimes barely perceptible illustrations.

Swanlund began her career like many of today's designers; she earned a bachelor of fine arts degree in 1986 from the University of Minnesota, then she *"stumbled"* into design work to make a living—though few probably milked goats and tended bar to survive between design jobs, as did she. Much of Swanlund's design during this time was done for editorial clients, including a stint with the prestigious literary magazine *Utne Reader*, where her work exhibited the classic, refined overtones of her fine arts training via balanced columnar layouts and clearly legible type arrangements. Recycled paper, minimal four-color usage, and few visual adornments also demonstrated Swanlund's empathy for the environmental movement, a major catalyst for many designers operating in the late 1980s.

Then, in 1990, Swanlund made a move that would significantly and forever change the way she thinks and works. She left the Midwest in pursuit of an MFA in design at the California Institute of the Arts (CalArts). While immersing herself in her studies, Swanlund taught design at the school and freelanced with some of the area's most progressive studios. She became deeply affected by the Golden State's spirit. She was especially intrigued by its plethora of odd characters and nonconformists, from her teachers at CalArts, whom she quickly adopted as mentors—people like ED FELLA, who preached that rules were meant to be challenged, bent, and broken—to her daily encounters with such quirky personalities as the accordion player who serenaded the traffic on Venice Boulevard and the woman who hobbled about Swanlund's neighborhood on stilts, *"her hair fashioned up into a single horn,"* Swanlund says. Their influence soon crept into her work, manifested in design arrangements that were as awkward, unbalanced, and illogical as the characters themselves. *"We live in a messy, ambiguous world with other humans, and my*

Sleepwalking, *1992.*
This is the second in a series of four panels Swanlund created to exhibit "ultimate image-making control over something that makes no sense." It was executed in Adobe Illustrator, Aldus FreeHand, Adobe Photoshop, and Analog, then assembled in QuarkXPress and screenprinted.

Terrorized by the past, tyrannized by the future, they
would rather recreate the world than play with the
rest of us.
My brothers are in the late stages of a deferred mid-
life crises. One works for a shrinking aerospace industry. Another deals with nuclear waste, designing ways
to imbed small bits of it into pea-sized bits of glass,
to be buried in remote places that no one cares much
about. Probably along Route 666. He could tell me
where, he says, but then he'd have to kill me.
Affectionate humor, he says. The last brother gave up
altogether, and lives in the woods,
because he doesn't
need to deal with
people there.

Despite
flamewars and stalkers
and the shrill scream
of a masculinity
that needs to redefine itself,
despite everything, there
are still dirt roads in CSpace,
where the rest of us live.
I travel these roads nearly all of my waking life, and lately,
into my dream-time as well. I am addicted, mostly.
It's a cheap and convenient repository for my angst and
self-loathing, my greed for wet, hedonistic pleasures,
tempered by paranoia of meat-borne viral beings.
It fulfills my need for consuming the interstices of
adventure and agency, cloaked, without needing to fear the
predators of the night, without needing my gun.
So with the Ducati and the warm pulse of electricity,
the umbilicus of technology moist between my legs,
I travel,
to sin and sin again
on the
Information Superhighway.

The end

Emigre #32, 1994.

Life's a Dream, 1994.

The CalArts School of Theater contacted Swanlund for a poster that shows how life is held together by tenuous threads. The designer considered it a perfect assignment, as she was engaged at the time in experimenting with deconstruction.

design work strives to reflect the way we live, see, and interpret," Swanlund explains.

Upon graduation in 1993, Swanlund joined *Emigre* magazine as a designer and occasional guest editor. Founders RUDY VANDERLANS and ZUZANA LICKO had established their magazine for the purpose of exploring design philosophy and its impact on society, as well as to provide a global forum for innovative design. At *Emigre* Swanlund retained aspects of her environmental sensitivity—minimal elements and earthy colors prevailed—but her compositions took on the incongruities of her California inspiration: a column might mutate into several widths on a single page; heavy rules might protrude into text for no apparent reason; visuals butted against columns of words; headlines were often hybrid mixtures of illustration and text. Her type treatments also demonstrated a shift in thinking. The refined, easily legible fonts of Swanlund's *Utne* days gave way to chunky, frequently ugly faces that sometimes required effort to decipher. Size and style of the text varied within an article, calling out passages to drive home the article's points. Design was no longer a passive vehicle for transferring messages in Swanlund's work; it became an equal partner with the words.

After two years at *Emigre*, Swanlund felt that she needed a new laboratory in which to continue her exploration, so she returned to Los Angeles and opened her own studio, SWANK. Today, her work still exhibits *Emigre*'s influence via its disparity of imagery, text, and spatial perspective, yet it also shows an even sharper rebellious edge, honed as much by her project choices as by her break from the design conventions of the Minnesota days.

Her work for *Snowflake* is a good example. This undoubtedly bizarre magazine is perhaps best described as a humorous, literary sex journal for winter sports enthusiasts. The cover of issue 2 is a visual culmination of Swanlund's California metamorphosis. The magazine's banner stretches across the top of the page in faded blue, snowflake-embellished letters set in GEOFF KAPLAN's eccentric font creation, Sucker, But. The banner appears as if it has been hand-stamped on the page. A crude, black-ink illustration of a snowflake (whose points are composed of scribbled words, eyeballs, and other odd doodles, à la Fella) spreads across the cover's center, creating a curious, yet simple decoration for the otherwise stark white background. Inside, the curious visage of Sucker, But,

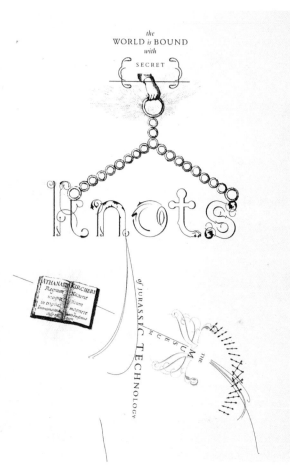

The World Is Bound with Secret Knots, *1997.*

This poster is a mixture of the expected—the series of knots that make up the "clothes hanger"—with the unexpected sense of off-balanced composition. The lettering in the word knot *displays an ornamental look that is evocative of wrought-iron railing.*

as well as GLEN NAKASAKO's Ligament and JONATHAN HOEFLER's Acropolis fonts are intermingled with the more editorially traditional look of Bimbo. Imagery throughout the magazine ranges from full-color photos of snow bunnies in action to primitive figures depicting mammoths, nippled mountains, Bigfoot, and dominatrixes. Visuals may or may not relate to the content of the articles they illustrate. Swanlund says of *Snowflake*'s design that she was *"trying to make something that is disorienting while still pretty, messed-up—but just subtly. . . . Perhaps a little bit tipsy like Ingrid Bergman in the opening scene of* Notorious.*"*

In spite of its frequently brazen appearance, Swanlund's work has begun to develop a sense of sweetness, too. This is especially evident in the poster she created for the CalArts School of Theater's productions of *Romeo and Juliet* and *A Midsummer Night's Dream*. Words dance lightly about the space, set in unassuming typefaces that are distinguished by playful touches such as the "crowning" of the final *o* in Romeo or the stacking of the *m*'s in *Midsummer*. The poster is visually eclectic by many design standards; nevertheless, it delivers its message effortlessly.

And that is a key to Swanlund's work. She believes that audiences are *"extremely visually literate"* and open to new ways of absorbing communication, but designers still have the obligation never to push their work beyond comprehension, no matter how involved they may become in their quest for individuality. *"A small amount of arrogance is nice,"* Swanlund says, *"but making useless work isn't really design. It still has to function in some sort of commercial arena."* The good news is, that arena is elastic and endlessly changeable.

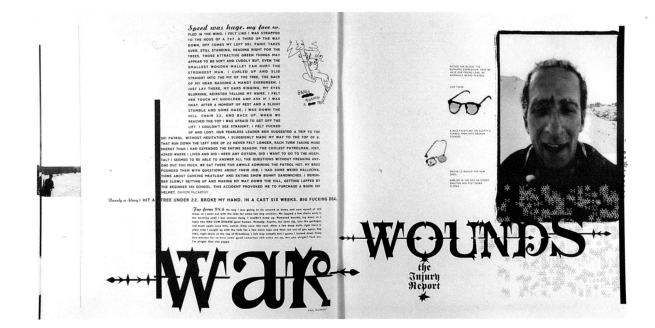

Snowflake, *1997.*

Snowflake is a magazine produced by two of Swanlund's writer friends focusing on an odd combination of snow sports and sex. Issue 1 (shown) covered everything from a comic discussing the virtues of Chicago's snow to "The Dyke Report," relaying a lesbian snowboarder's humorous experiences on the slopes. Swanlund's design is as frivolous as the editorial content, incorporating outrageous illustrations and photography, whimsical type treatments, and an eclectic selection of fonts ranging from medieval to cartoon lettering.

giulio turturro

Verve Records, New York, New York

stimulate!

GIULIO TURTURRO believes that the best design stimulates not just the eye, but also the mind of the viewer. His keen appreciation for concept is partially a result of his previous career in illustration, where he was required to synthesize the gist of a subject into a single potent image. He also credits much of his fresh approach to CHARLES GOSLIN, his teacher at the Pratt Institute, from which Turturro graduated in 1984. Goslin encouraged Turturro to think about his work, not just use design to decorate. Today, Turturro's commitment to concept is so strong that he remembers an art director's directive to *"just make a project look good, don't worry about the idea"* as the most insulting remark ever made regarding his work. *"I believe you should give viewers their money's worth. Once you've drawn them in, give them something to remember when they leave,"* he explains. Ideas are indelible *and* timeless.

As art director of Verve Records, which produces alternative and classic jazz and blues albums, Turturro's designs run the gamut from establishment to avant-garde, according to the style of the musicians for whom he is creating. Mostly, though, it leans to the latter, a combination of layered type and strong palettes intermingled with natural and accidental imagery. A collection of old tins, for example, adorns the cover of a Shirley Horn album, injecting it with an emotional nostalgia. In another CD, the words in a New York subway's directional sign are cleverly replaced with the title of Christian McBride's album, *Number Two Express.* The subway's directional arrow is repeated on the CD itself, with the striking, yet simple black icon making a powerful statement against the white background.

The same visual expressiveness that Turturro sought in illustration becomes his starting point for each design assignment. A CD cover he created for blues musician John Scofield's first Verve album offers a good example. The album, which featured acoustic selections of Scofield's music, was appropriately titled *Quiet.* So Turturro hit upon the idea of shooting a photo of Scofield in a library and using that as the cover's main element. *"There is a second, not-so-obvious reason for the library, too,"* Turturro adds. The walls of the library were

John Scofield, Quiet, *1996.*

New Releases, July 1996.

The designer used the Fourth of July's most recognizable images, then added an unexpected touch by incorporating Chinese firecrackers.

The Jazz Divas, *1996.*

Turturro wanted to appeal to a contemporary audience and focus on the important parts of singing—the mouth and the microphone—for this CD compilation. He created a star shape in Adobe Illustrator to communicate the status of the selected artists. The duotone photo was placed in the star, also using Illustrator, and images were then scanned in through or manipulated in Adobe Photoshop.

covered in wood, which picked up the wood tones in the acoustic guitar Scofield holds in the photo. Next, Turturro searched for a way to offset the *"quiet"* look of the library with a *"little noise."* He found his solution in an erratic placement of type and imagery, giving the package a contemporary disposition.

In recent years, Turturro has found that he is expanding beyond his reliance on imagery to count more and more on typography in delivering his ideas. He greatly appreciates the computer for how it has allowed designers to develop a virtually unlimited menu of fonts (he views such typography as yet another form of abstract expressionism), which enables him to always find—or create—one to match his subject's personality. For example, he used the expressive face Matrix on the album *Wave: The Antonio Carlos Jobim Songbook*. Matrix promotes the album's Latino character, aided by energetic colors and playful, almost geometric figures.

When Turturro entered the music packaging arena in the late 1980s, he couldn't help but be influenced by DAVID CARSON, NEVILLE BRODY, and VAUGHAN OLIVER, especially for how they injected personal views into their work using iconographic type. He also admired how they could detect a design solution in an accident, such as turning a shadow that resulted from a dirty photocopier into a critical visual element. Conversely, Turturro appreciates the legacy of PAUL RAND and LESTER BEALL, who helped make graphic design a legitimate art form. Rand's work in the latter half of the twentieth century is characterized by its wit, simplicity, and a Bauhaus approach to problem solving, and many of the logos he designed—especially for IBM and Westinghouse—are design classics. Beall was a pioneer in the modern design movement, introducing many avant-garde concepts to American designers before the influx of European design immigrants in the late 1930s.

Rand and Beall, in effect, changed how design is perceived—which Turturro believes is the true measure of a Radical. He hesitates to consider himself one for that reason. However, Turturro's conceptual sagacity has already positioned him squarely under design's intense spotlight.

Christian McBride, Number Two Express, *1996.*

Wave: The Antonio Carlos Jobim Songbook, *1996.*

Turturro, seeking to relay the exotic, tropical feel of Jobim's music, incorporated images connoted by Jobim's songs—beautiful women, nature, the beach, and so on—then selected a playful typeface to match the illustrations. Many of these visual elements are also applied to other CD designs in the Jobim Songbook *series.*

Shirley Horn, **The Main Ingredient,** *1996.*

selected bibliography

BOOKS

American Center for Design. **The 100 Show: Design Year in Review.** Chicago: American Center for Design, 1994.

Blackwell, Lewis. **20th Century Type.** New York: Rizzoli, 1992.

Brody, Neville, and Jon Wozencraft. **The Graphic Language of Neville Brody.** Vol. 2. New York: Universe Books, 1996.

De la Croix, Horst, and Richard G. Tansey. **Art Through the Ages.** New York: Harcourt, Brace & World, Inc., 1970.

Livingston, Alan, and Isabella Livingston. **The Thames and Hudson Encyclopaedia of Graphic Design + Designers.** London: Thames and Hudson Ltd., 1992.

Meggs, Philip B. **A History of Graphic Design.** 2nd Ed. New York: Van Nostrand Reinhold, 1992.

Poynor, Rick, and Edward Booth-Clibborn. **Typography Now, The Next Wave.** London: Booth-Clibborn Editions, 1991.

Walker Art Center. **Graphic Design in America: A Visual Language History.** New York: Harry N. Abrams Inc., 1989.

Wild, Lorraine. **"Notes on Edward Fella: Design in a Bordertown."** In *Looking Closer 2: Critical Writings on Graphic Design.* New York: Allworth Press, 1997.

ARTICLES

Heller, Steven. **"The 1960s: Mainstream and Counterculture."** *Print* 43, no. 6 (November/December 1989): 11–37.

***HOW* magazine,** various issues, 1990–98.

Jacobs, Karrie. **"Katherine McCoy: On Modernism, Post-Modernism, Evolution, & Fate, Marking the End of an Era at Cranbrook."** *AIGA Journal* 12, no. 2 (1994): 27–29.

Plagens, Peter, and Ray Sawhill. **"The Font of Youth."** *Newsweek,* February 26, 1996: 64–65.

Simko, Alison. **"Do the Left Thing.**" *Creativity,* January 12, 1992: 22–32.

Smartner, Bob. **"Retropective: High Performance Design in a Smog-Restricted Era."** *Emigre* 38 (1996): 20–23.

Tomkins, Calvin. **"Dada and Mama."** *The New Yorker,* January 15, 1996: 56–62.

Triggs, Teal. **"Flux Type."** *Eye* 2, no. 7 (1992): 46–55.

VanderLans, Rudy. **"Emigre Talks with the Founder of The Designers Republic, Ian Anderson."** *Emigre* 29 (1993): 4–20.

Wilhelmson, Brenda, and Terry Kattleman. **"Thirstysomething."** *Creativity* 1, no. 3 (1993): 20–29.

All rights and copyrights for the illustrations in this book are maintained by the original copyright holders
and licensees. All efforts have been made to provide proper copyright attribution
to the artwork appearing in this
book.

Pg. 16, *Ray Gun*, © 1993 Ray Gun Publishing; pg. 17, Esse ©1991 Gilbert Paper; pg. 20, The Times They Are a Changin' ©1996 Cross Pointe Paper Corp.; pg. 23, "It's Newt" ©1995 Guerrilla Girls; pg. 25, Fluxshop ©1984 Rick Gardner; pg. 26, "Let's get Butt-Naked and Write Poetry" ©1996 Plazm Media Inc.; pg. 28, The Velvet Underground, *Live MCMXCIII* ©1993 Warner Bros./Sire Records; pg. 29, The Museum of Television & Radio Web site and schedule concepts ©1996 Museum of Television & Radio; pg. 48, Lou Reed, *Magic and Loss* ©1992 Warner Bros./Sire Records; pg. 49, The Velvet Underground, *Live MCMXCIII* poster ©1993 Warner Bros./Sire Records, Talking Heads, *Cities* ©1979 Sire Records, New York Gold, Volume 10 ©1997 New York Gold Inc.; pg. 62, *The Classical Language of Architecture* ©1969 MIT Press; pg. 63, Cranbrook Academy of Art poster ©1975 Cranbrook Academy of Art; pg. 64, Cranbrook catalog ©1979 Cranbrook Academy of Art; pg. 65, *Cranbrook Design: The New Discourse* ©1990 Rizzoli International, Cranbrook Ceramics poster ©1987 Cranbrook Academy of Art (photography ©1987 Steven Rost); pg. 70, Enter ©1989 American Center for Design; pg. 71, Add a Little Magic ©1992 Scitex, Give and Take ©1993 Gilbert Paper; pg. 72, Fisher Bicycle catalog ©1996 Gary Fisher Mountain Bikes; pg. 86, The Orb, *A Huge Ever Growing Pulsating Brain that Rules from the Center of the Ultraworld* ©1989 The Designers Republic/Wau!, Mr. Modo Records; pg. 87, Pop Will Eat Itself, *This Is the Day . . . This Is the Hour . . . This Is This!* ©1989 The Designers Republic/RCA Records, Pop Will Eat Itself, *16 Different Flavours of Hell* ©1993 The Designers Republic/BMG Records; pg. 88, Work, Buy, Consume, Die ©1995 The Designers Republic/Pho-Ku Corp.; pg. 89, Age of Chance, *Who's Afraid of the Big Bad Noise! Remix* ©1987 The Designers Republic/Virgin Records, Moo ©1996 The Designers Republic/Federation; pg. 90, Dual Layer Metal Coating ©1998 The Designers Republic/Sony; pg. 93, Power Voice logo ©1997 Power Voice, Converse catalog ©1995 Converse (product photography © Peter Rice, location and model photos © Butch Belair); pg. 94, TDK mailer ©1995 TDK; pg. 95, Magic Hat Ale ©1994 Magic Hat Brewing Company, Edward Mayer poster (photography) ©1996 Edward Mayer; pg. 110, Now Time ©1994 Now Time; pg. 111, PowerPhone poster ©1997 iMagic Infomedia Technology Ltd., *Metropolis*, "Championing the Verb" ©1996 Bellerophon Publications Inc.; pg. 112, Reprise Records logo ©1994–1996 Reprise Records; pg. 113, BBDO Worldwide Web site ©1996 BBDO, CalArts Bulletin ©1996 California Institute of the Arts; pg. 114, Excite, Are You Experienced ©1996 Excite Inc.; pg. 115, *Wired*, "Language as Creation" ©1999 The Condé Nast Publications Inc., Avalon Hotel identity and signage ©1999 Avalon Hotel; pg. 130, Techweenie ©1996 Type Directors Club; pg. 131, Eaglethon poster ©1996 Harley-Davidson Inc.; pg. 132, Smoking Popes, *Destination Failure* ©1997 Capitol Records Inc., Ministry, *Filth Pig* ©1996 Warner Bros. Records; pg. 133, *Luna, Bella Luna* ©1997 Paul Elledge; pg. 134, Theater Zeebelt ©1993 Studio Dumbar; pg. 136, *Ray Gun*, "Stand by Your Man" ©1992 Ray Gun Publishing; pg. 137, *Speak* covers ©1996, 1998 Speak Magazine; pg. 138, CCAC card ©1995 California College of Arts and Crafts, Reebok Exhibit ©1998 Reebok International Ltd.; pg. 139, *Bordertown* ©1997 Chronicle Books; pg. 140, Next directory ©1990 Why Not Associates (photography ©1990 Rocco Redondo); pg. 141, *U&lc* ©1996 Why Not Associates (photography ©1996 Rocco Redondo); pg. 142, Royal Mail of Britain Olympic stamp presentation pack ©1996 The Royal Mail; pg. 144, Barbican Arts Centre, "Monsters of Grace" poster ©1998 Why Not Associates (photography ©1998 Rocco Redondo and Photodisc), Barbican Arts Centre, "[OR]" poster ©1998 Why Not Associates (photography ©1998 Rocco Redondo and E. Valette); pg. 145, "Disturbanisms" ©1997 Why Not Associates (photography ©1990 Rocco Redondo and Photodisc); pg. 146, *The Art of Mickey Mouse* ©1993 Disney, *The Art of Barbie* ©1995 Mattel Inc.; pg. 147, *Big Boy* ©1996 Elias Bros.; pg. 148, Rock & Barf *MuSICKal* Instruments ©1997 Yoe! Studios;

pg. 149, Cartoon Network brochure ©1997 Turner; pg. 152, *Ray Gun* ©1997 Ray Gun Publishing; pg. 153, *Interference* ©1993 Ümran Projects, *Blah, Blah, Blah* ©1996 Ray Gun Publishing and MTV Europe; pg. 154, *2xIntro* ©1998 Little, Brown and Company; pg. 155, *Creative Review* ©1996 Creative Review, Robbie Robertson, *Contact from the Underworld of Redboy* ©1998 Capitol Records; pg. 164, *Huh* spread ©1996 Ray Gun Publishing; pg. 165, *Huh* cover and spread ©1996 Ray Gun Publishing; pg. 166, *Sweater* logo ©1997 Ray Gun Publishing; pg. 167, *Bikini* cover and spread ©1997 Ray Gun Publishing; pg. 168, *Form + Zweck* nr ©1995 Cyan (photography ©1995 Baron de Meyer); pg. 171, Lucia Moholy ©1995 Cyan (photography © Lucia Moholy); pg. 172, Bauhaus-Block Von Mischa Kuball ©1992, 1993 Cyan (photography © Peter Latzen); pg. 178, Atlantic Olympic Committee bid books ©1990 Atlanta Olympic Committee; pg. 179, Divitale promotions ©1993 Divitale Productions Inc., Violence and the Crucifixion of Innocence ©1994 Black Book Marketing Group; pg. 181, The Only Way Out ©1993 Black Book Marketing Group; pg. 182, *Impulse,* "Primal Scream" ©1994 Anchorage Daily News; pg. 183, *Impulse,* "Make Room" ©1993 Anchorage Daily News, *Impulse,* "Soul Music" ©1994 Anchorage Daily News; pg. 184, MSNBC Web page ©1998 MSNBC; pg. 185, MSNBC Web page ©1998 MSNBC, "8" ©1994, 1995 Anchorage Daily News; pg. 188, "Intersections and Interstices" ©1996 Cranbrook Academy of Art; pg. 189, Cranbrook Academy of Art catalog ©1996 Cranbrook Academy of Art; pg. 191, Cranbrook Academy of Art Museum invitation ©1995 Cranbrook Academy of Art; pg. 192, *Jamming the Media* ©1997 Chronicle Books; pg. 194, *Multimedia Graphics* ©1995 Chronicle Books; pg. 198, Pro-Pain, *The Truth Hurts* ©1994 Energy Records; pg. 199, The 4-A's ©1992 The 4-A's, YMO CD covers ©1993 Toshica/EMI; pg. 200, Sonny Sharrock, *Into Another Light* ©1996 Enemy Records, *Fresh Dialogue* ©1996 AIGA New York; pg. 201, Lou Reed poster ©1996 Warner Bros. Records Inc.; pg. 210, Shakespeare poster ©1994 CalArts School of Theater Arts; pg. 212, *Emigre #32* ©1994 Emigre; pg. 213, "Life's a Dream" poster ©1994 CalArts School of Theater Arts; pg. 214, "The World Is Bound with Secret Knots" poster ©1997 The Museum of Jurassic Technology; pg. 215, *Snowflake* ©1997 Smart Art Press; pgs. 216–219, ©1996 Verve Records.